Guide to **LEED**® 2009

ESTIMATING AND PRECONSTRUCTION STRATEGIES

Guide to
LEED® 2009

ESTIMATING AND
PRECONSTRUCTION
STRATEGIES

WILEY

John Wiley & Sons, Inc.

THOMAS A. TAYLOR,
LEED BD+C,
Alberici Group, Inc.

This book is printed on acid-free paper.♾

Copyright © 2011 by John Wiley & Sons, Inc. All rights reserved

Published by John Wiley & Sons, Inc., Hoboken, New Jersey
Published simultaneously in Canada

Wiley also publishes its books in a variety of electronic formats. Some content that appears in print may
not be available in electronic books. For more information about Wiley products, visit our web site at
www.wiley.com.

Library of Congress Cataloging-in-Publication Data:

Taylor, Thomas A., 1964-
 Guide to LEED 2009 estimating and preconstruction strategies / Thomas A. Taylor.
  p. cm.
 Includes index.
 ISBN 978-0-470-53371-0 (cloth); ISBN 978-0-470-90252-3 (ebk); ISBN 978-0-470-90253-0 (ebk);
 ISBN 978-0-470-90254-7 (ebk); ISBN 978-0-470-95037-1 (ebk); ISBN 978-0-470-95061-6 (ebk)
  1. Sustainable buildings—Design and construction—Estimates. 2. Leadership in Energy and
 Environmental Design Green Building Rating System. I. Title.
 TH880.T39 2011
 720'.47—dc22
                                                                      2010030984

Printed in the United States of America

10 9 8 7 6 5 4 3 2 1

Contents

PART I

Introduction

CHAPTER 1

Establishing Parameters

Before beginning a discussion about sustainable design and construction, we must narrow the scope of the conversation. While assembling the information for this book, the contributors collectively agreed that before a discussion of estimating and preconstruction of a sustainable or "green" project can proceed, several parameters must be defined, as each project is unique. Some owners use a prototype building model that has been proven time and time again, an experience that allows them to use a "cookie cutter" approach when delivering subsequent buildings. The contractors working on these projects will agree that the building components, materials and assemblies may be the same, but each project will have different constraints. Issues regarding requirements of the local municipality, seasonal effect on scheduled activities, availability of manpower, and possibly different subcontractors all can make each "cookie cutter" project distinctive.

For this reason, the contributors of this book feel it is necessary to establish a framework in which the discussions and examples are provided. It is the intent of the contributors to share information regarding the processes used to plan, estimate and execute a sustainable project. We have included case studies of projects that represent a cross-section of building types. These projects represent different geographical locations and levels of certification under the U.S. Green Building Council's (USGBC) Leadership in Energy and Environmental Design (LEED®) Green Building Rating System. Our experience indicates that the problems, risks, and lack of understanding on projects are essentially the same regardless of what rating system is being used on a project. As LEED is the most widely used rating system in the United States, we have chosen to focus on projects delivered under the various LEED rating systems. We have also included examples to illustrate the impact that LEED requirements have on contractors. We include examples of extreme events that have impacted contractors in the past. It should not be inferred that these situations are the norm; rather they are provided to inform contractors of the potential effects that sustainable projects can have.

We want the reader to understand that there are several things that will influence the outcome of a LEED project, and in particular this information is intended to help contractors understand the LEED 2009 for New Construction rating system. Those of us in the construction industry know that no two projects are the same. The information in this book can be applied as one possible way, but not the only way, of estimating and producing a preconstruction plan for a project seeking LEED certification.

TERMS

Green building is a relatively new wave in the construction industry that has brought many new terms and phrases: green, green buildings, sustainable buildings, high-performance buildings, integrated design, zero net energy, integrated delivery, living buildings, regenerative design, and the list goes on. What do all of these terms mean? This may be the most difficult question to answer because these terms have different definitions depending on whom you ask. Often you will see these phrases used to define one another, and still others in the industry will mix and match these phrases as the way to explain a design or a building. Consider these passages, for example:

> A green building, also known as a sustainable building, is a structure that is designed, built, renovated, operated, or reused in an ecological and resource-efficient manner. Green buildings are designed to meet certain objectives such as protecting occupant health; improving employee productivity; using energy, water, and other resources more efficiently; and reducing the overall impact to the environment.

> California Integrated Waste Management Board

Most people would agree that a green building must be an energy efficient building.

EnergyStar

In the first example the terms "green building" and "sustainable building" are used to explain each other. In both examples, the definitions equate these buildings to the efficient use of various resources. The first example leads a reader to believe that the construction of a green/sustainable building results in less environmental impact while protecting the health of the building occupants, while the second focuses mainly on energy efficiency. The prevalence of definitions illustrates why there is so much confusion about green building. We will not attempt to debate the pros and cons of the multitude of definitions of green buildings. Instead we will set our first parameter: for the purposes of this book, we will define a "green" or "sustainable" building as one that has used the U.S. Green Building Council's LEED Green Building Rating System.

RATING SYSTEMS

There are a variety of green building rating systems. Depending on what statistic is used, there are as many as 100 different programs worldwide and even more if you include guidelines and protocols in addition to the complete ratings systems. In the United States, the LEED rating systems are used as well as the Green Building Initiative's Green Globes self-assessment and certification tool. There also are strong local programs such as the Austin Energy Commercial Green Building Program and Rating Tool, the State of Minnesota Sustainable Building Guidelines (Version 2.1), and the New York City Department of Design and Construction's *High Performance Building Guidelines*. For residential construction, the USGBC offers LEED for Homes, the National Association of Home Builders has a National Green Building Standard, and there are many local programs such as the Atlanta-based program EarthCraft House. LEED and Green Globes both have their roots in international programs such as Go Green and the BRE Environmental Assessment Method (BREEAM). Teams that are new to the green building industry can quickly become confused when looking for the best or most applicable rating system for their projects. The LEED rating system, which is nearly ubiquitous in the U.S. market and is used internationally, will be the focus of this book.

LEED was developed by the U.S. Green Building Council (USGBC). Founded in 1993, USGBC's stated mission is "to transform the way buildings and communities are designed, built, and operated, enabling an environmentally and socially responsible, healthy and prosperous environment that improves the quality of life." LEED is a point-based system made up of prerequisites and voluntary credits. These prerequisites and points are distributed in seven distinct categories addressing:

1. Site issues: Sustainable Sites (SS)
2. Water conservation: Water Efficiency (WE)
3. Energy conservation: Energy and Atmosphere (EA)
4. Building materials and products: Material and Resources (MR)
5. Occupant comfort and health: Indoor Environmental Quality (IEQ)
6. Innovation: Innovation in Design (ID)
7. Regionalism: Regional Priority (RP)

The LEED 2009 for New Construction system contains eight prerequisites necessary for any level of certification. Projects must then achieve enough voluntary credits to be awarded one of four possible levels of certification: Certified, Silver, Gold, and Platinum.

USGBC has stated that the LEED rating system was created to provide third-party verification that a building or community was designed and built using strategies aimed at improving performance across all the metrics that matter most: energy savings, water efficiency, carbon dioxide (CO_2) emissions reduction, improved indoor environmental quality, and stewardship of resources and sensitivity to their impacts.

Since the time of the initial launch of LEED-NC, USGBC has expanded the LEED rating system into a suite of products:

LEED-NC	New Construction and Major Renovation
LEED-CI	Commercial Interiors
LEED-CS	Core and Shell
LEED-EB	Existing Buildings: Operations and Maintenance
LEED-Homes	Homes and low-rise residential structures
LEED-ND	Neighborhood Development
LEED-Schools	Educational buildings designed for kindergarten through twelfth grade

The latest iteration of the LEED program, LEED Version 3, made several changes to the administrative process and standardized the point scale across all rating systems to 100 base points with a total of 10 additional points available in the optional Innovation in Design and Regional Priority categories. Each of the systems remains unique to a particular building type or function. The newest version of the rating systems is called LEED 2009. The variety of LEED rating systems provides our second parameter: we will focus this book on the LEED 2009 for New Construction rating system. We will not examine detailed information regarding the other rating systems within the suite of LEED products. There may be times when examples within this work draw upon a project team's experience working on LEED projects other than LEED-NC. We have included those examples to illustrate common issues a contractor may face while working on a project seeking LEED certification.

CHAPTER 2

The LEED Rating System

The LEED rating systems were developed by USGBC to be used on a voluntary basis by any team working on the construction or renovation of a project. Throughout the life of the project, the team designs, constructs, and documents activities that demonstrate compliance with the criteria set forth by the applicable LEED rating system.

LEED VERSION 3

On April 27, 2009, the USGBC introduced LEED Version 3 (v3). This LEED upgrade created the latest edition of the overall LEED green building rating system known as LEED 2009. Any project registered after the effective date of the introduction of the revised program is required to certify under LEED 2009. The prerequisites and credits discussed in this book follow the most current version of the rating system, LEED 2009 for New Construction. Due to LEED 2009's recent release, much of the information contained in the case studies is based on older versions of the rating system.

The changes incorporated into LEED 2009 are, for the most part, performance enhancements rather than substantive changes.

Prior to the introduction of LEED v3, each of the various rating system products had separate reference manuals and point systems. Under LEED v3, USGBC:

- Sanctioned the Green Building Certification Institute (GBCI) to perform all project reviews
- Authorized the GBCI to manage the Accredited Professional credentialing program
- Established a Policy Manual and Terms and Conditions for the use of the LEED rating system
- Updated and standardized the point scale for all LEED rating systems
- Consolidated the seven individual reference manuals into three works

Reference Manuals

The LEED Reference Manual has always been the "go-to" guide for direction while working on a LEED project. Separate reference manuals for each of the rating systems had to be purchased, creating extra expense and materials for LEED project teams. The LEED v3 initiative established consolidated information into three guides focused on commercial- or institutional-type buildings with separate guides for homes and neighborhood development.

Green Building Design and Construction

This manual combines information on three rating systems: LEED for New Construction and Major Renovations (LEED-NC), LEED for Core and Shell (LEED-CS) and LEED for Schools (LEED-Schools). Eventually, this manual will include information on two additional rating systems: LEED for Healthcare and LEED for Retail. Following is a more detailed description of the project types covered by this manual.

LEED 2009 for New Construction was designed largely for new commercial office buildings. However, LEED-NC can be applied to a wide range of building types. LEED-NC defines new construction as a new building created on a greenfield or previously developed site. Additions to existing buildings can also qualify under this system whether or not the existing building is renovated. A major renovation is defined as involving substantial HVAC modifications, major envelope changes and significant interior renovation.

LEED-CS applies to core and shell projects where the building shell and limited amounts of the building core will be constructed and the finishes to the tenant spaces (those outside of the core) will be the responsibility of the tenant.

LEED-Schools is specifically for projects in schools serving kindergarten through twelfth grade.

Certification under any one of these rating systems is considered a one-time event. Once construction is complete and certification is awarded, there is no requirement for recertification; however, USGBC strongly encourages these building owners to continue sustainable practices through enrollment in the LEED Existing Buildings: Operations and Maintenance program. Whether or not recertification is pursued, a building owner must provide detailed information regarding the building's energy and water use to USGBC/GBCI for a period of time defined by the Minimum Program Requirements or face having their building decertified.

Green Building Operations and Maintenance

This manual contains information on LEED for Existing Buildings: Operations and Maintenance (EB O&M). This program applies to a building that has been operational for at least two years or when planned renovations will displace less than half of the occupants of the building. LEED-EB O&M requires recertification on a biannual basis.

Green Interior Design and Construction

This manual contains information on LEED for Commercial Interiors (CI), which applies to tenant fit-out projects. The tenant is responsible for the interior portions of a building, in part or in total, but not the construction or renovation of the building's core and shell.

LEED ONLINE

When USGBC launched Version 2.2 of the LEED for New Construction rating system, they modified the certification process and began requiring all teams to utilize their LEED Online tool for all correspondence and documentation transfer pertaining to a specific project. USGBC's development of this computer-based program streamlined the process of project certification, and in concept, the development of this tool was a positive change when compared to the previous process of paper, or "hard copy," submissions. The LEED portion of the project, including registration, documentation, process management, submission, and certification reviews are conducted online using the LEED Online web site and user interface. After the project was registered, the team used the system to track anticipated credits and review prerequisite and credit documentation uploaded to support the submission at the end of the project. The LEED Online tool allowed the Project Administrator (the person who registered the project) the ability to communicate to members of the team regarding all of the various aspects of a LEED project. The online tool also allowed a team to access credit interpretation requests and rulings. Credit interpretation requests (CIRs) allowed project teams to submit a LEED specific question pertaining to their project to a LEED Technical Advisory Group (TAG). Inquiries had to be specific to the application of prescribed requirements of a prerequisite or credit within the rating system. Responses to those questions were provided in written format and could be used as a basis for documenting achievement of that specific credit or prerequisite. All questions asked by previous project teams were collected in a searchable database that could be accessed by team members working on a project registered through the online system. CIRs and rulings thereby created precedent for all future projects that might encounter a similar circumstance.

USGBC launched the Green Building Certification Institute (GBCI) in January of 2008 as a third-party project certification body and credentialing authority. One of the GBCI's primary roles is in the administration of the LEED certification process. LEED Version 3 introduced changes to both the LEED rating system and the LEED Online system. LEED Online was upgraded to improve the speed, capacity and ease of use. This update to the existing LEED Online system is one example of how USGBC and GBCI seek to continually improve not only the rating system but its related processes and tools to keep pace with the demands of the marketplace. The original LEED Online was launched and advertised as a management tool for project teams, streamlining the documentation, review, and certification process. Those of us who labored through the launch and subsequent debugging of the original LEED Online system understand the importance of these recent upgrades.

When LEED Online was first introduced, there were a number of problems with the programming, support, and processes. Over time, the problems that earlier users encountered diminished. However, frequent users of the online tool are all too aware of the problems that still existed within the original program. The most significant of the problems was in the way a LEED Project Administrator was required to upload documents required for project submission. While LEED Online was created in an effort to move the documentation process to a paperless system, the process was far from paperless. In its barest essence, the LEED Online tool was structured as an electronic filing cabinet. It created a place where a team could store documents that would eventually be provided to the GBCI for submission and review. Project teams generating paper documents had to convert them into electronic documents prior to each upload. There was a common misconception that when a project team was ready to submit their documents for review, they simply hit a button and the submission was sent. In actuality, the LEED Project Administrator or other project team member was still required to assemble each of the documents required for submission and upload each one separately.

Terms and Conditions

In addition to the consolidation of the reference manuals, USGBC and GBCI have made many substantial changes to the conditions for using the LEED rating systems. These changes come in the form of obligatory language that an owner and those team members who use the rating system must adhere to if they wish to certify a building or project.

Components of LEED Version 3

LEED v3 is an evolutionary step towards providing users with a flexible rating tool while incorporating new building sciences technology and advancements. The new version of LEED also establishes a priority on building energy efficiency and the reduction of CO_2 and other greenhouse gas emissions. Specifically, LEED v3 incorporates three general components:

- LEED 2009

    Technical advancements to and standardization of the prerequisites and credits contained within the LEED rating systems; USGBC will also issue quarterly addenda that make routine updates to the rating systems
- LEED Online

    An upgrade to LEED Online that reflects changes made in LEED 2009 and allows for a faster and easier to use system
- Certification model

    An expanded certification infrastructure based on International Organization for Standardization (ISO) standards, administered by the Green Building Certification Institute (GBCI) for improved performance as well as speed and capacity of certification reviews

LEED Online and the Preconstruction/ Contractor Team

With the advancements of the LEED Online system, the process of submitting a project for certification has become more efficient. Even with these enhancements, the process of documenting and submitting a project for review still takes a significant amount of time. Depending on the size and complexity of a project, the effort required to document and upload the construction-related prerequisites and credits could add significant hours to a contractor's general conditions. If the contract documents for a project do not specifically call out who is responsible for the upload of required documentation to LEED Online, then the contractor should ask the question or clarify that this administrative function is not a part of their scope of work.

LEED 2009: Technical Advancements

The LEED for New Construction system under LEED 2009 has eight prerequisites and 110 credit points. LEED Version 2.2 contained seven prerequisites and 69 available credits. A team must achieve all prerequisites and adequate credit points to achieve the following point thresholds:

- 40–Certified
- 50–Silver
- 60–Gold
- 80–Platinum

The majority of the credit requirements have not changed. However, the allocations of the points have been modified to better reflect new building science technology and an emphasis on the reduction of greenhouse gas emissions. For example, the points within the Sustainable Sites category have been reallocated from one prerequisite and 14 credit points in LEED Version 2.2 to one prerequisite and 26 credit points in LEED 2009. Alternative Transportation, the section of the rating system that awarded points for promoting bicycle use, reduction of parking, use of alternative fuel vehicles and carpooling, is now worth more points although the basic premise for the requirements of these credits remains the same. The reallocation of points thereby rewards a building owner for the resulting reduction of greenhouse gas emissions due to a reduction of automobile use. In the Energy and Atmosphere (EA) category, LEED Version 2.2 had three prerequisites and 17 credit points. In

LEED 2009, there are 3 prerequisites and 35 credits in the EA category. This change rewards a building owner for reductions in energy consumption, which in turn reduces greenhouse gas emissions related to energy production. These changes are an important step in creating more energy efficient buildings.

LEED Process

The following sections will detail the LEED process and explore both the changes brought about by LEED v3 as well as their impact to the construction process.

LEED REGISTERED PROJECTS

A construction project that is registered with USGBC only indicates the team's intent to certify the project. An online form containing basic project information is submitted and payment is made to USGBC.

LEED PREREQUISITES

There are certain requirements or activities that must be completed on a project in order for it to become LEED certified. These prerequisites for certification carry no associated points, but teams must successfully achieve and document all prerequisites if they intend to certify the project. LEED 2009 for New Construction has eight prerequisites, each of which will be addressed in detail in Part II of this book.

- SSp1: Construction Activity Pollution Prevention

    This prerequisite is governed by the U.S. Environmental Protection Agency requirements under EPA-832R-92-005 Chapter 3 or local code, whichever is more stringent.
- WEp1: Water Use Reduction Projects must achieve a 20 percent reduction in potable water use.
- EAp1: Fundamental Commissioning of the Building Energy Systems

    Commissioning services must be provided by a qualified and experienced commissioning authority.
- EAp2: Minimum Energy Performance

    Projects must meet American National Standards Institute (ANSI), American Society of Heating, Refrigerating, and Air-Conditioning Engineers (ASHRAE) and Illuminating Engineering Society of North America (IESNA) Standard 90.1-2007.

- EAp3: Fundamental Refrigerant Management

    Project equipment must utilize no chlorofluorocarbon (CFC)-based refrigerants.

- MRp1: Storage and Collection of Recyclables

    A recycling program must be established for paper, glass, plastics, cardboard and metals at a minimum.

- EQp1: Minimum Indoor Air Quality Performance

    Projects must meet the requirements of ASHRAE Standard 62.1-2007.

- EQp2: Environmental Tobacco Smoke (ETS) Control

    Projects must employ measures to ensure zero exposure of nonsmokers to ETS.

LEED CERTIFIED PROJECTS

A project cannot be certified by USGBC/GBCI until design, construction and commissioning activities are completed and all documentation has been collected and formatted in a manner that satisfies the requirements of the various LEED prerequisites and credits. The documents are then reviewed by USGBC/GBCI and provided that all prerequisites have been met, awards a level of certification based on the points achieved.

Certification Process

The team may submit their project in one or two phases. Teams submitting under the one phase process collect all required documentation as the design and construction occurs during the project. Upon completion of the construction activities, project teams submit their work for review by USGBC/GBCI. Teams submitting under a two-phase process first submit the design-related prerequisites and credits at the completion of the design phase. No points are awarded at this phase of submission; they are instead anticipated or denied. Upon completion of construction, all credits (design and construction) are submitted for review. Only after construction and final review of a project can a project become LEED certified. Any information offered before the completion of construction is preliminary and conditional.

In both the one- and two-phase submission process, the project team assembles the necessary documents to demonstrate compliance with all prerequisites and credits prior to submission and review by USGBC/GBCI. The reviewers then respond with initial comments. The project team has a specified number of days to respond to those comments and submit supplemental information in support of their project

Implications of Two-Phase Submission

It should be noted that the two-phase submission may provide an opening for some participants in the project team to shed responsibility for the final outcome of a project. We have observed situations in which the design-related credits were reviewed by the GBCI and deemed "anticipated" prior to the start of construction. At completion of construction, it was left to the contractor to document all of the credits (to verify the design and document the construction). In cases where documentation for a particular design credit had changed during construction, the contractor had to create new documents in an effort to complete the project submission. The design team interpreted the conditional acceptance of their work by USGBC/GBCI as final acceptance and any alteration to that work after the design phase review was seen as additional in scope, requiring additional compensation. The contractor incurred additional unanticipated costs at the end of the project in order to get the project certified by USGBC.

submission. The reviewers evaluate the final information and return an offered level of certification. Upon receipt, a team can accept or appeal the final offer. Acceptance results in a certification. A team may also appeal one or more of the final decisions of the LEED reviewer. An appeal involves submission of additional documentation and subsequent review before final certification is achieved. No project is certified until the review body has offered, and the team has accepted, the certification level for the building.

Reviewers

Prior to the launch of LEED 2009 and the creation of the GBCI to administer the process, the USGBC review process was somewhat subjective. The consultants hired by USGBC were professionals in the design and engineering disciplines and had different areas of expertise. While there was a high level of knowledge and experience within the firms hired by USGBC to perform project certification reviews, there was at times, a subjective bias to the review. For example, we have worked with a project team to complete two very similar projects. Common elements of these projects were the owner, designer, construction management team, use of the buildings, size, layout, equipment, and materials. The difference between these two projects was only site location. When the consultant prepared and submitted the projects to USGBC for review, they received differing comments. There were similarities, but credit points that required further clarification were distinct and did not relate to the variance in site locations.

The changes in the LEED certification review methodology are perhaps the most significant modification to come about through LEED 2009. Though the process itself does not follow ISO protocols and has not been standardized under ISO, the new process is based on ISO standards. In addition, the consultants recruited and hired by the GBCI to perform LEED v3 reviews are ISO-certified organizations.

A Word of Caution

The GBCI has taken over administration of the certification process from USGBC in an effort to improve the return time of certification reviews, as well as their consistency and quality. Project teams using previous versions of the system for review and certification have experienced as much as three- to four-month delays in certification. However, in their endeavor to accelerate the process, the GBCI is allowing alternative submittal methods that, if not careful, may diminish the rigor of the LEED name. Under the new certification process, a team may elect to use a team member's professional designation or professional license (i.e., stamp) in lieu of submitting supporting documents that demonstrate credit compliance. From a time management standpoint, this option may appear to be an enhancement to the documentation and review process. Rather, with the growing list of municipalities that mandate certification, the shift from proof of compliance through actual documentation and evidence to a professional status, seal or stamp could prove to have a negative result. Under LEED v3, a project could be decertified if allegations are made, investigated and validated that a team did not design and document the requirements of any particular prerequisite or credit properly. These challenges will typically occur after the project has been completed. If a professional stamp is used to document a credit, the drawings, calculations and design information will be absent from the project records. This lack of information will require additional time and resources to research and possibly create the documentation needed to refute a challenge. Additionally, without documentation, a reviewer could miss any mistakes or subjective decisions a professional may make.

For example, the ISO certified firms hired by the GBCI have demonstrated experience in the certification of individual products; however, their employees are not necessarily professionals in the design and construction of commercial buildings. The LEED rating system utilizes several commonly recognized industry standards as a basis for its requirements. Depending on the situation, these standards can be left to the interpretation of the professional attempting to demonstrate compliance with their requirements in the design of a building or its systems. An example of this is

ANSI/ASHRAE/IESNA Standard 90.1 is the default standard for minimum energy performance for a building seeking certification under the LEED rating system. This standard suggests that each room in a building should incorporate motion sensors for lights so they automatically turn off when not occupied. The standard provides clear direction to the designer as to when to use a motion sensor. However, the standard does not provide clear direction as to what a "room" is. In one case, a bathroom stall may be built with full height drywall and a locking door. Are these areas to be interpreted as toilet stalls or rooms? It is up to the designer to determine whether motion sensor light switching is required. The Standard may be clear but the interpretation of the term "room" is not. If this scenario is put into the context of the professional putting forward his or her credentials in lieu of documentation, no third party is reviewing the documentation to evaluate whether the professional's *interpretation* of the standard is correct.

ADMINISTRATIVE CHANGES TO LEED

The LEED 2009 changes were enacted to keep pace with the needs of the marketplace. These changes are not limited to the credit requirements and point allocations within the rating system. In addition, there have been significant changes to the process of using the LEED rating system itself. A dramatic change is that all entities in the LEED process must agree to conform to new requirements contained in several documents:

- Policy Manual
    This manual establishes the Minimum Program Requirements for project eligibility.
- LEED Certification Terms and Conditions for Project Registration/LEED 2009
- Terms and Conditions for LEED Online
- Certification Agreement between Green Building Certification Institute and Project owner

These agreements restrict and obligate each member of the team: owner, designer, contractor, end user and even the future purchaser of a LEED certified building. These obligations should be understood by all members of the project team at the outset of the LEED project so that, at a minimum, they can be incorporated into the appropriate contract documents. We will examine these obligations in detail later in this book.

Specifications

Contractors looking to get involved with LEED projects need to understand the difference between a product and a performance specification in order to recognize that what appears to be a product specification may actually be a performance specification. Our experience has indicated that when a project is offered as a design-bid-build delivery, it is to be awarded in a low-cost and competitive process and that the specifications are intended to be a product-based one. However, the lines between the types of specifications tend to blur on LEED projects. The requirements of LEED introduce performance criteria into the specifications and these requirements change the product specification into a performance-based specification. This change adds a level of complexity to the estimating and pre-construction activities of a project in addition to the risk and liability associated with contract compliance.

Product Specification

A product specification is most commonly used in delivering a design-bid-build project. Typically, the specifications incorporate a selection of acceptable products that are to be used in the delivery of a project. The purpose of a product specification or a product-based specification is that no design is required by the contractor estimating or delivering the project. The product specification provides a list of acceptable products to be used on the project in every category of work covered by the specification. This document becomes the basis of the contract after final award has been made. Performance criteria for any category of work are provided in the event the contractor chooses to offer a substitution for those products included in the document.

Performance Specification

A performance specification is used when it is the contractor's responsibility to identify products that fulfill certain design criteria included in the specification. No (or very few) products are offered as a list of acceptable products in this type of specification. Because of the design choices the contractor must make in this type of specification, it is typically used in design-build or design-assist delivery of a project. A contractor who accepts a performance-based specification is aware that more time and effort will be put forth during the estimating and preconstruction phase of the project. In many cases, there will be some design or decision making performed by the contractor or their subcontractors and consultants.

Specifications and the Preconstruction/Contractor Team

When looking at a specification, the preconstruction/contractor team should pay special attention to the general specification section titled "LEED or Sustainable Requirements." Nearly all LEED projects that are delivered under a design-bid-build methodology will include a section of the specifications that is similarly titled. The specification numbering system used to identify this section can vary but the information contained in this section of the contract documents rarely changes. Most often these requirements are found in the 01 section of the specification along with other general or specific items required by the contractor, their subcontractors, and suppliers. When performing the preconstruction tasks on a LEED project, it is critically important that all proposing contractors and suppliers read and understand the requirements of this and all other general conditions of the contract.

Contractors need to be aware that specifiers have varying degrees of knowledge of and experience with LEED and that poorly written specifications for a LEED project can add significant risk for the construction firm. A review of more than 20 sets of specifications indicates that the specification writers in the sampling had little to no knowledge of the LEED criteria. Furthermore, the writers seldom expended the energy to ensure that all specific language, materials, and assemblies were in accordance with the general requirements found in this section of the specification. In more than ten of the reviewed cases, the term "LEED" was only included six times in the entire body of the general section of the specification (excluding the specific section). This indicates the LEED requirements were not integrated into the specification; rather, they had been added into the specification with little or no forethought.

In today's fast-moving and competitive market, those in the architecture, engineering and construction (AEC) industry look for a way to lower cost and improve profitability. Design firms often turn to packaged software programs to assist in the creation of their specifications. These programs now include the capability to create a "LEED" or "Sustainable" specification with a keystroke. However, as in the case with the development of an estimate for a LEED project, it takes a much greater knowledge base of the actual LEED rating

(Continued)

system to achieve success. In all cases, certain statements should immediately alert a contractor to the significance of the LEED requirements:

Section includes general requirements and procedures for compliance with certain USGBC LEED prerequisites and credits needed for the project to obtain LEED-Certified certification based on LEED.

Other LEED prerequisites and credits needed to obtain LEED certification depend on the material selections and may not be specifically identified as LEED requirements. Compliance with requirements needed to obtain LEED prerequisites and credits may be used as one criterion to evaluate substitution requests and comparable product requests.

Additional LEED prerequisites and credits needed to obtain the indicated LEED certification depend on Architect's design and other aspects of project that are not part of the work of this contract.

In the above cases, the contractor is asked to take responsibility for material selection regardless of what has been outlined in the specification. Some may take exception to this assertion and comment that this is only true if a contractor plans to make a substitution to a specified product. This may or may not be the case and depends largely on the diligence of the designer to ensure that all products listed in the specification will meet the performance and monetary thresholds set by the LEED requirements, regardless of the combination of products that the contractor chooses to base their successful low bid upon.

Pay close attention to appendices or attachments:

A copy of the LEED project checklist is attached at the end of this section for information only.

A contractor should be cautious when a LEED project checklist is included in the specifications, even if the specification indicates that it is for "information only." Once a piece of information is included in the specification, it becomes a contract document. After all, isn't the entire specification issued for information purposes? The LEED project checklist indicates which prerequisites and credits a design team intends to achieve through the delivery of the project. Once this document is made a part of the contract documents, it can become a binding agreement of the individual credits and prerequisites being sought by the team. This can obligate a contractor to performance-related items that are not expressed throughout the documents.

Blanket statements, like this one, imply responsibility:

Related Sections: Refer to the following sections for related work:

Divisions 1 through 16 Sections for LEED requirements specific to the Work of each of those Sections. These requirements may or may not include reference to LEED.

(Continued)

This statement informs the contractor that regardless of what is included in the specifications; it is the contractor's responsibility to know what is required by the LEED prerequisites and credits. The contractor assumes the responsibility to furnish the materials, systems, or assemblies required to meet those LEED requirements. Statements like the one above should be of great concern to a contractor. Additional requirements may be associated with the work described in any particular specification section even if they are not specifically identified.

ACTION PLANS AND PROGRESS REPORTS

Specifications for a project seeking LEED certification will in almost all cases require the contractor to submit additional LEED-specific documentation and reports. Often, this LEED-related information is in the form of action plans and progress reports.

Action Plans

The action plan is intended to provide specific information about how the contractor will achieve points and prerequisites found in the LEED rating system. The most common credits to be included in action plans are MR Credit 2: Construction Waste Management, MR Credit 4: Recycled Content, MR Credit 5: Regional Materials, IEQ Credit 3.1: Construction Indoor Air Quality Management Plan—During Construction, IEQ Credit 3.2: Construction Indoor Air Quality Management Plan-Before Occupancy, and IEQ Credits 4.1 through 4.4: Low-Emitting Materials. Action plans are generally required to be submitted within a specified amount of time following the award of the project.

Progress Reports

Progress reports are required on a month-by-month basis and are usually required to be submitted with each pay application made by the contractor. There are three types of progress reports that correspond with specific credits for materials, construction waste management and indoor environmental quality.

Reports on material-related credits provide detailed information about the building materials and products purchased for the project. Progress reports for MRc4: Recycled Content and MRc5: Regional Materials are two common examples. Occasionally, depending on the project's credit point goals, progress reports for MRc6: Rapidly Renewable Materials and MRc7: Certified Wood will also be requested.

These reports require specific information about the cost of each item used on the project, excluding mechanical equipment, electrical equipment, plumbing systems, vertical transportation, and furniture in some cases.

Progress reports for MRc2: Construction Waste Management require information about the amount of construction and demolition (C&D) waste leaving the site and the disposition of those materials (i.e., recycled, donated or landfilled).

The contractor may also be responsible for submitting progress reports for other LEED categories, including Energy and Atmosphere and Indoor Environmental Quality. Progress reports for credits falling into these categories require information from the contractor during the process of delivering a project. Examples include EAc5: Measurement and Verification, IEQ Credit 3.1: Construction Indoor Air Quality Management Plan—During Construction, IEQ Credit 3.2: Construction Indoor Air Quality Management Plan—Before Occupancy and IEQ Credits 4.1 through 4.4: Low-Emitting Materials.

Example

The following example illustrates how the completion of action plans and progress reports can be a critical to a contractor's success on a LEED project. The LEED requirements in a project's specification call for the contractor to produce an action plan for how they will achieve the LEED credits MRc4: Recycled Content, MRc5: Regional Materials, MRc7: Certified Wood, and IEQc4.4: Low-Emitting Materials—Composite Wood and Agrifiber Products through performance standards. The wood door specification offers five door manufacturers that are acceptable and listed in the product specifications. In a non-LEED project, the contractor would choose the door that is listed in the specification and also achieves the lowest cost on bid day. However, on the LEED project, the contractor is required to look for the low-cost solution while simultaneously making a judgment as to which of the products listed in the specification will also be in accordance with the performance standards mandated by the LEED requirement on the project.

The contractor will be asked to produce and submit LEED action plans prior to commencement of work. However, if a contractor starts this process during the estimating and preconstruction phase of the project, the LEED action plans can be submitted very early in the process, which will aid in determining whether the thresholds established in the rating system can be met based on the materials listed in the specifications.

Project Delivery Type

The delivery method for any given construction project depends on an owner's preference and experience. It is rarely affected by the owner's decision to pursue

LEED certification. LEED projects can be certified using all of the conventional delivery methods, which are described in more detail in the following sections.

Construction Manager as Agent

Owners using this delivery method hire a construction manager (CM) to act as their agent. The CM may be responsible for preconstruction estimates, assembly of bid packages, project construction schedules, and overall site management. However, under this delivery method, the owner holds all contracts with the contractors or suppliers working on the project.

Construction Management at Risk

In this type of delivery method, the CM enters into a service contract with the owner. The CM will then enter into contracts with all required specialty contractors and suppliers sufficient to carry out the scope of work identified in the contract documents. Under this delivery model, the firm acting as the CM is at risk for the completion of the project. There are many variations to this delivery model (often called CM/GC), and can be contracted under a hard bid or negotiated scenario.

Design-Build

An owner will select this delivery method when they wish to bundle the entire delivery of a project into one package. The owner will select one design-build firm who will be responsible for both the design of the project and the construction. As with the other delivery methods, this method has several variations.

Design-Bid-Build

This is probably the most widely used of all of the delivery methods. Under this delivery system, the owner selects a team to design the building. Once the design is complete the contract documents are offered to the market for a competitive bidding process. Under this delivery, an owner will typically choose the contractor with the lowest qualified bid to perform the scope of work based on cost.

A Word of Caution

This "low-bid" mentality in a design-bid-build project delivery does not typically bring out the best in a firm. This delivery method can start a project off with a group of adversaries instead of a team with a common goal. It reinforces a defensive posture that leads to members of the team relying solely on the information offered in the contract documents. A contractor might say that if "it" is not included in the four corners of the contract documents, then you are not getting "it." To which the architect may respond that if the contractor was any good, they would understand the intent of the design. This last example may be extreme but many professionals in the industry that have competed in a hard bid market will likely have witnessed this attitude at least once in their career.

A Third Parameter

The definitions of project delivery type provide us with the third parameter for this work. We will assume throughout this book that the delivery of the project will be under the design-bid-build delivery method. We have chosen this as our model delivery type primarily because it is often the most popular method for delivering green buildings and is the delivery method most owners prefer. This popularity comes not necessarily from the delivery method's success, but primarily from its use on publicly funded or government projects that typically require competitive bids for each division of work. USGBC has been very successful in their efforts to establish the LEED rating system into legislative language. This has afforded the LEED system a place in most government contract requirements. At the time of this work, there are 14 federal, 34 state, and 243 local green building policies, most of which require LEED certification for projects over a set dollar value.

Estimate

In the construction industry, an estimate is the declaration of the approximate amount to be charged for a particular scope of work a firm or person submits. In a design-bid-build project, the estimate is based on the quantity of material and labor required to complete the task. The accuracy of the estimate will depend on the information furnished in the contract documents. If the information is ample and provides clarity, the estimate will typically be accurate. The key to a contractor's success on this type of project is the quality of the contract documents. Poorly written and inaccurate information in the contract documents will result in a high number of requests for information (RFIs) during and after the project's bidding phase.

Unfortunately, in a competitive construction market the low bid gets the job. Equally unfortunate is the basic misconception that the design-bid-build process will provide the best result. Not all design teams vet the products, materials and assemblies included in their design to fulfill an owner's needs in terms of quality and price. A design-bid-build project relies on the drawings that have been issued for construction and a product-based specification.

Following are several examples of problems project teams have encountered in construction documents:

- Products listed in specifications that are no longer manufactured.
- Details of construction assemblies that cannot be constructed.
- Information that is contrary to building codes.
- Materials contained in the specifications that are inconsistent with one another
- Conflicts with materials or their applications that could potentially void manufacturer's warranties.

In the above examples, the contractor bears the risk of inadequate, vague, or erroneous design information. The contractor is forced to make decisions that affect price, liability, their profit, and the possible satisfaction of a client. This is because the owner is operating under the premise that the design will produce the building that is expected, at a cost that has been estimated usually by someone other than the contractor performing the work. In most cases, the owner's experience with project delivery is limited and trust has been placed in the members of the delivery team with whom they have built a relationship. Generally, that relationship is established long before the contractor is even selected for the project. If a problem arises with the estimate, who is the owner going to believe—their partner over the past several months or the contractor who just entered the team?

Estimating and Preconstruction Activities

On any project, the estimating activities are based on the quantities of material and assemblies described in the construction documents. The material, assemblies, and equipment needed for the project are described in a product specification. Execution of the work is left to the know-how of the contractor. On a hard bid project, the person performing estimating activities is forced to rely on the contract documents to create the proposed cost of the work. The products that are listed in the specification have been called out by manufacturer name or other means of specific identification, and a contractor will typically use various specified materials in a variety of combinations that will result in the lowest price on bid day. A contractor wishing to use some manufacturer other than those included in the specification must request a substitution to the contract documents. The process of performing a quantity survey and then soliciting prices for material and services is straightforward. However, a talented estimator goes beyond the simple functions of quantity survey. An experienced estimator uses his or her knowledge to determine if additional time or resources will be required to meet the individual circumstances of the project. This experience can be the key factor in winning the project and making a profit. When an estimator goes beyond the simple pricing of a quantity of material, they are practicing effective preconstruction activities. An estimate is not complete if items of general conditions, schedule, workforce, sequence of work, documentation, and project closeout are not addressed. Leaving these items out of the bid price could win you the project, but at what future cost?

Just as knowledge and experience can work to an estimator's benefit, knowledge, and experience can sometimes work against an estimator or contractor. For example, let's assume a contractor has a good working knowledge of the needs of an owner's staff based on past experience and other projects. The contractor knows that this particular owner will require coordination meetings to be conducted twice weekly. The level of detail that is required for reporting at these meetings is extremely high and the owner's representative will not be satisfied with anything less. The project specifications require the contractor to attend coordination meetings. However, the specifications do not stipulate the frequency of those coordination meetings. In this situation, the contractors competing for this work have never worked for this owner before and assume from their past project experience that coordination meetings occur weekly. What is the knowledgeable contractor to do? Adjust the price to reflect the time and effort that will be required to satisfy the owner? Or base the price on what the competitors will do? Should the contractor write an RFI regarding the amount of meetings that will be required? Or ignore past experience and price what is in the specifications? The manner in which these questions are answered will affect how the estimator prices the project.

- If you price what you know is going to be required, your price will probably be higher than your competition and you will not be awarded the contract.
- If you price what is in the documents you may end up spending more money than what is included in the estimate.
- If you price and deliver only those services that you feel are specifically called out in the specifications, you may risk an unsatisfied client.

Another example: A contractor is compiling the estimate for a design-bid-build project. The estimator performs the quantity survey for the door and hardware assemblies indicated on the drawings. The estimator reviews the specification and knows that of the five hardware manufacturers listed in the specifications, only one has consistently provided the lowest price. The estimator also knows that many owners' level of satisfaction with this hardware is very low.

- Does the estimator apply his knowledge and include the higher cost hardware?
- Does the estimator provide the lowest price on bid day regardless of the potential satisfaction of the owner?

Similar pitfalls may be evidenced on LEED projects as well. Estimators working on a project seeking LEED certification may find themselves performing more work than on a non-LEED project. The estimate for a LEED project includes all of the activities found in a non-LEED project along with the requirements of the prerequisites and credits being sought for certification. The main difference between estimating for a LEED project and a traditional project is that the estimate for a project seeking LEED certification should be performed by an estimator who is knowledgeable in construction means and methods, the requirements of the LEED rating system and how the various credits within the rating system are interrelated.

Contractors competing in the green building market should have an estimator on staff who has experience with the LEED rating system. Knowledge of the LEED system is critical because when the requirements of LEED are applied to a project, layers of complexity are added to its execution. The contractual responsibilities of team members are often unclear, leaving room for broad interpretation of the contract documents. As discussed above, the product-based specification relied on so heavily in design-bid-build work, is now complicated by performance requirements set in place by the LEED criteria. The requirements of LEED often change the specifications from product-based to performance-based. Changes to the basis of the specification should trigger a change to the approach taken during the estimating phase of the project.

There are many similarities and differences between the preconstruction/estimating of LEED projects and non-LEED projects. For example, a team that hopes to achieve MR Credit 4: Recycled Content and MR Credit 5: Regional Materials typifies the dual nature of many LEED projects. MRc4 rewards up to two points for sourcing materials made with high amounts of recycled content, while MRc5 rewards up to two points for the use of regionally extracted and manufactured materials. The quantity survey of materials in the design is conducted in the same manner as any other project. However, on the LEED registered project, the products that have been included in the specification cannot be evaluated based on price alone. The estimator must assess every combination of products or materials listed in the specification to determine which combination will fulfill the LEED requirements and then match that information to the lowest cost solution. An estimator cannot trust that the author of the specification has accounted for the LEED requirements in every product combination. In this example, the amount of recycled content in each product or material, the manufacturer location of the product or material and the location of extraction of the product's raw materials all become vitally important. The product specification has turned into a performance specification. This transformation forces the contractor to assume the responsibility to look at price as well as the product's contribution to the LEED effort. This example becomes even more complex if the contract documents indicate that in addition to recycled content and regional sourcing, the project also seeks to achieve IEQc4.1 through 4.4: Low-Emitting Materials. The requirements of these four credits require the contractor to consider these performance standards as well as the two credits previously mentioned. We will explain the requirements of each of these credits in greater detail later in this book. This example is offered as a way to demonstrate the intricacy of estimating and preconstruction activities when working on a LEED project.

An estimator with little or no experience with the requirements of the LEED rating system will not be able to predict the success of the project, nor will he or she be able to properly price the materials and labor that are required on a project seeking LEED certification. Estimators can take three attitudes toward a project aspect that is new or unfamiliar. They can ignore what they do not know and act like it is just like every other project they have estimated. They can add a cost premium to complete the work, either by a percentage or by a line item addition and hope it is enough to cover any surprises during the project execution. Or they can ask the questions during the bidding phase and potentially expose a competitive edge they have against competitors. This "pick one of the three" approach may work when you are talking about a single aspect of a project, perhaps a particular finish detail in one room, but a lack of knowledge regarding the LEED requirements is an entirely different story. The performance requirements of the LEED prerequisites and credits touch almost all aspects of project execution. Not knowing the requirements of the rating system may prevent a contractor from being in full compliance with their contract. For example, failure to understand how the performance requirements affect material choices can force a contractor to spend additional money during the procurement phase. Another example is that the neglect of the implied duties of management and administration of the commissioning process can force a contractor to add staff to their field management team. Additionally, a supplier's lack of understanding of the documentation process can cause the loss of a credit point due to missing information and thus diminish the possibility of certification.

The estimator on a LEED project must formulate a plan for project execution. Preconstruction planning is critical because the estimate has to include a strategic plan that is in compliance with the product specification's LEED requirements. Ignoring these requirements or assuming that the general sustainable requirements have been integrated into the entire specification is dangerous. It adds to the risk associated with the contracting process.

After reading this, some contractors might ask, "Why would I ever want to take on a project like this?" The answer is that in most commercial building markets, the green building movement is continuing to show strength despite hurdles in implementation. In 2008, McGraw-Hill Construction presented information at the Associated General Contractors of America's annual conference. They indicated that by the year 2013, the market for green buildings will be between 96 and 140 billion dollars annually. In that same presentation, they reported that from 2005 through 2008, the green building market for construction grew fivefold. Additionally, by 2013, 82 percent of contractors will be building green on at least 11 percent of their projects (McGraw-Hill Construction, 2008[1]). A contractor who continues to provide services in commercial or residential construction will eventually be asked to build to a green or sustainable standard.

---

1. McGraw-Hill Construction. (2008). *Key Trends in the European Market and U.S. Construction Marketplace: SmartMarket Report*. McGraw-Hill Construction.

CHAPTER 3

Before You Start

There are as many reasons why an owner wants to certify buildings under USGBC's (U.S. Green Building Council) LEED rating system as there are certified buildings. Owners decide to build green based on corporate peer pressure, demonstration of their stewardship of the environment, operational cost savings through energy reduction, shrinking their carbon footprint, or just because they want to "do the right thing." Depending on the project location, the choice may be based on a government mandate to build green. Between 2005 and 2008, the number of individual states that had some sort of "green" legislation grew from 57 to 156. (McGraw-Hill Construction, 2008[1]).

Before a building owner makes the decision to go green or possibly have a building LEED certified, he or she should ask, "Does having a green building make sense for my organization?" If the decision to green the facility comes with too many negative implications, it will not be the most sustainable solution. The decision to go green must be made by each individual owner for each individual project. Equally

---

1. McGraw-Hill Construction. (2008). *Key Trends in the European Market and U.S. Construction Marketplace: SmartMarket Report*. McGraw-Hill Construction.

Case Study

An organization grows beyond the capacity of its current office. The organization's board of directors commits to build a new building. The chief executive officer (CEO) challenges the design and construction teams to find the "best" solutions for their new building. Her use of the word 'best' is not referring to the most expensive solution; instead, she encourages the team to examine what the industry has to offer and to find the most applicable solutions for the project. This CEO believes that building a new building for the firm is a rare opportunity, so it is imperative to investigate and evaluate all of the possibilities. In researching the various delivery methods one of the team members suggests the possibility of using the LEED rating system as a framework for the new project. After a presentation to the board, the CEO decides that going green is the right thing to do. However, she gives the team some very specific deliverables:

1. The project must be built under the same budget as a conventional building.
2. The design must be respectful of the organizational needs of the company.
3. If the project is going to seek certification under USGBC's LEED rating system, they will aim for the highest level, Platinum.

The CEO decides to go green because she realizes that the people working for the firm are the most precious asset, and following the intent of the LEED rating system will result in a building that reflects a core principle of the company. She feels that the building itself will demonstrate that the company cares for its employees by providing them the best working environment possible.

The challenge to deliver a LEED Platinum building at the same cost as a conventional non-LEED building begins as a daunting task. As the design progresses, the team discovers that every choice they make affects the outcome. Using the LEED system as a guide, the team continually looks for ways to maximize the amount of points that can be earned. This quest leads the team to a growing understanding that the building has to be designed as a system, not a collection of separate components. At project completion, the team delivers the project within budget and on time, and achieves Platinum certification. The CEO, the board, and the employees are all very pleased with the building. Shortly after occupancy, the CEO discovers that in providing the firm with the best building possible, they also receive benefits that were not factored into

(Continued)

the equation in the beginning. The firm is recognized with industry awards for the design and the construction. The community appreciates the efforts, evidenced by multiple requests for tours of the facility. The chief financial officer, who was skeptical of the decision to go green, realizes that there are true operational savings in the utility bills. There is a tremendous reduction in sick days. The CEO originally made the decision to go green for one reason but clearly realized many other benefits.

important, however, is that there are many reasons for pursuing sustainability and no particular reason is better than another. When owners make the decision to go green, they will reap the benefits of the other reasons to build in a sustainable manner.

WHERE TO BEGIN?

The process of designing a building is foreign to most owners. They require assistance in taking their thoughts and ideas and putting them onto paper. An owner must ask the right questions before starting. Traditionally, a project begins with a need or a desire to create a new space. After choosing to invest in a new building, an owner usually turns to an architect for guidance and help framing the vision. The architect will then typically create renderings that give an owner a good idea of what the building will look like. The process of turning an idea into a building image can be complex. An architect may wish to get to know the owner, the organization, and the expectations for the project. The architect may interview key people in the organization to understand their space needs, may look at an organization's growth plan, and will work with the real estate brokers to see what type, shape, and size building may fit on a prospective parcel of land. No matter how or by what path the architect uses, he or she comes up with one or sometimes multiple drawings of what the building might look like. Once an owner has seen what the new building will look like, he or she seldom looks back. After the conceptual design is approved, the design proceeds, culminating in a set of drawings and specifications that can be offered to the construction market for competitive quotes for the construction of the building. When looking to create a LEED building, the owner seldom follows a different path.

When starting on a project, owners trust that the architect they have selected has the knowledge and the experience to provide a design for a building that satisfies their needs. Unfortunately, there are more people who think they know how to deliver a LEED building than have actually delivered a LEED-certified building. Between 2000 and 2005, only 167 buildings were certified by USGBC, with 1,772 projects registered but failing to complete the certification process (Schendler & Udall, 2005[2]). At the time of this work, there are 5,787 LEED certified and 27,515 LEED registered commercial projects. Ten years of data reinforces the fact that there are still very few design and construction professionals with the experience necessary to deliver a LEED certified project to successful completion.

It is important to understand everything it takes to complete one of these highly specialized buildings. When looking at the number of buildings that have been built over the past ten years, less than 6,000 have become LEED certified. Why is there such a large gap between those who register buildings with USGBC and those who actually achieve certification? The answer is simple: it takes a lot of work to get a building certified!

The Team

The success of any project is dependent on the strength of the team assembled to deliver the project. A LEED project differs from a non-LEED project in that all members of the delivery team must understand their responsibilities and rise to a standard that will achieve the outcome desired by the owner. On a LEED project the core team of the owner, architect, discipline engineers, contractor, subcontractor, and operator of the building must understand that they have a role to play in the success of a LEED certified building. Each member of this team has distinct roles and responsibilities. On a LEED project the work of each team member needs to be considerate of each discipline because in a sustainable building, each system has a significant impact on the others.

For example, the architect creating the look of the exterior must understand how his or her work will impact the energy efficiency of the building. The discipline engineers must look at each building as a new challenge and not use a standard design that may add redundancy to the system. The contractor and subcontractors must understand the impact that they have in constructing a LEED certified building. Care must be taken when selecting and installing materials. Operators of a LEED building must understand that they cannot run the building in a reactive way that only addresses immediate problems. They must operate the building as it was designed or they will not achieve the energy cost reductions that were predicted during the design phase.

An individual member of the team may have detailed knowledge and experience with LEED projects, but it is the strength of the team that will enable success. In the real world, not every team is going to be made up of members that have a great deal

---

2. Schendler, A., and R. Udall. *LEED is Broken . . . Let's Fix It*. Aspen CO (2005).

of experience with the LEED process. In cases where there is little knowledge, the members of the team must be willing to learn and support each other by taking an active part in the delivery of the project.

To deliver a certified building, everyone on the team—owner, architect, discipline engineers, contractor, subcontractors, suppliers, and operator—must understand the effect they have on the finished product. Everyone has to view the team with great respect and be willing to take on the responsibility that comes with designing, constructing, owning, and operating a LEED certified building.

For example, let's take the following hypothetical example. An owner makes a decision for a new building to become LEED certified. A request for qualifications (RFQ) is sent out to several architectural firms. Part of the request mentions that the project is to become LEED certified but the level of certification is not mentioned because the owner does not have enough experience to understand what may be possible. The owner receives two strong proposals.

Architectural Firm A relishes the opportunity to work on a LEED project. In the past, the firm was always in a position where they had to "sell" LEED concepts to the owner.

Architectural Firm B responds that they have a certain amount of LEED Accredited Professionals (APs) on staff and that they have worked on 15 LEED projects.

The owner reviews the responses and, based on the information provided, perceives that Firm B has more experience. The owner assumes that if Firm B has worked on 15 LEED projects, then they must know what they are doing and will understand the owner's motivation for certification.

The firm that responded that it has worked on 15 LEED projects is selected for the project.

In this hypothetical situation, the owner may have asked for references and general information used to assist in validating the response. However, the owner never clearly stated the goals in asking for a LEED building, nor did the owner ask the important questions about this firm's stated experience:

- Are the 15 LEED projects registered or certified?
- In each of the 15 projects, what certification level did the owner originally target and what certification level was ultimately achieved?
- What was the cost of the building?
- Will subconsultants be utilized on the project, and if so, how much experience do they have with LEED buildings?
- Who actually performed the tasks involved with getting the project certified?
- How many change orders were issued from the end of design to the completion of construction?

Most owners do not know enough about the process to ask these questions. As we discussed, owners tend to trust the professionals they hire for their projects. When these professionals tout their experience, they are seldom questioned. Trust based on an assumption or perception can lead to problems and disappointment in the long run.

Cost

Cost is always a question when investigating LEED. The most common question is, "How much more does it cost to do LEED?" Some of the cost of LEED can be found on the USGBC or the Green Building Certification Institute (GBCI) web sites and consists of project registration and certification fees. When looking at the typical project's overall budget for a midsize building (approximately 50,000 square feet), these fees are viewed by most teams as a manageable expense and are not out of line proportionately. Other fees involved with LEED certification include commissioning and energy modeling costs, as well as possible administrative and consulting fees. Owners who are inquiring about the cost of LEED have most likely heard stories from other people that in order to produce a LEED building, they spent a lot of money. Some may even use the information they have heard to validate why they do not want to pursue LEED certification. When an owner asks how much it costs to have a LEED building, think about another question: "How much more than what?"

There are many examples of LEED buildings that cost 10, 20, and up to 100 percent more than a non-LEED building. However, there are also examples in which LEED-certified buildings have cost the same or nearly the same as their more conventional counterparts. The building has to be defined before a cost can be determined. Some of the technologies available to achieve the desired intent of the LEED credits admittedly may be expensive; however, those choices and credits are optional. When discussing cost, it's important to distinguish between a cost attributable to an optional choice and one that is attributable to a requirement necessary to achieve even the most basic level of certification.

There are items and activities that must be included with the delivery of a LEED project that are not usually found in a non-LEED building. These items will have additional costs associated with them:

- USGBC registration and certification filing fees
- Energy modeling (depending on the size of the building) and information on the targeted energy efficiency

- Commissioning of the energy using systems in the building
- Documentation of the design and construction activities for certification

Beyond these items, most if not all of what will be encountered in a LEED project will be the same as a non-LEED project. Depending on the ability of the team, these costs can be funded within a traditional budget. With effort, a project can become certified with little to no additional cost.

Change Orders

Whether or not a project is seeking LEED certification, change orders are costly. Changes to a project, especially after construction has commenced, will slow down a project, add frustration to the team, and cost money. If a change is incorporated early in design there is very little impact to the overall cost of the project. The later a change is made, regardless of the size of that change, the more impact it will have on the project and the higher its cost will be. Equilibrium is found on or about the time that the construction documents are complete.

Case Study

A mechanical design calls for Minimum Efficiency Reporting Value (MERV) 13 filters to be installed in all of the air-handling equipment. The design team feels that this is a good way to achieve LEED IEQ Credit 5: Indoor Chemical and Pollutant Source Control. While equipment using MERV 13 filters supplies cleaner air to the occupants as compared to a system equipped with a lower MERV-rated filter, the filters are larger and more costly. Additionally, the fan size of the equipment must be increased to accommodate the static pressure caused by the thickness of the filter. Additionally, IEQc5 calls for several other design elements to be a part of the building besides the filter size. If the team misses one of the other elements, then the point cannot be achieved. These other considerations include an entry walk-off system at least ten feet in length, enclosed copy centers, and dedicated exhaust for all locations where chemicals are mixed or stored. In the early stage of construction, the contractor places the order for the air handling equipment to accommodate MERV 13 filters. After the order is placed, it is discovered that the copy rooms are not enclosed and the building is going to have no entry mat or

(Continued)

vestibule. Because the other required elements were not made a part of the early design, the team must decide whether to:

- Enclose the copy centers, incorporate dedicated exhaust, and add a vestibule and walk-off entry system to the entrance of the building, or
- Stop the order for the air-handling equipment and reorder the equipment to accommodate a smaller filter, which will compromise the schedule, result in the equipment being resized, and change the structure for the roof-mounted curbs. In addition, the LEED point is lost.

In the end, the team chooses to enclose the copy room, change the exhaust ductwork, and incorporate an entry vestibule with a walk-off mat. The change is very costly to the owner, but the owner values the increased quality of the air that is delivered in the building. At completion of the project, the team begins to document the credits. It was at this time that the mechanical engineer reread the LEED requirements and discovered that the MERV 13 filters were required not only in the fresh air intake, which was incorporated into the design, but also on the return side of the equipment. The system was not designed to accommodate filtration on both sides of the equipment. The team could not document this credit and the point was lost, in spite of the extra effort from the team. Had the team members understood all of the requirements at the time of the design, the equipment and systems could have been included from the beginning, the point would have been achieved and costly changes would have been avoided.

CHAPTER 4

LEED Process

PHASED SUBMISSION

USGBC continues to make enhancements to the LEED rating system in an effort to streamline the certification process and to make the system more appealing to owners, designers, and contractors. USGBC has watched the building industry closely and when speculative building owners commented that the LEED-NC Rating System was not suited for speculative core and shell-type projects, USGBC reacted. They introduced a rating system specific for core and shell projects, LEED for Core and Shell (LEED-CS). This rating system provides certification opportunity to developers who work with tenants responsible for their own finishes or build-out. This new product also created a two-part project submission. The two-phased project submission for LEED-CS projects allows an owner the ability to "precertify" their building prior to construction. This precertification allows the building developer to presell or lease space in what will be a certified building once it is constructed. Subsequently, the two-phased project submission process was incorporated into the other LEED rating systems. However, only in the LEED-CS system is there an option for an actual precertification. Projects in all other rating systems are given conditional approval for submitted and reviewed design phase prerequisites and credits. Prior to this change, all projects were required to complete the design, construction, and commissioning activities of a building before project submission.

Registered versus Certified

Many designers rely on specification writing software and data files to aid in the development of contract documents. These subscription-based software and data file tools provide the designer with a database of information to create the project specifications. Many of these tools now include modules for sustainability and LEED-related language. However, in the hands of an inexperienced team, the use of these tools can provide erroneous and vague language leaving the responsibility of who is to document and sometimes even achieve certain LEED credits open to interpretation. Often, these specifications will require the contractor to evaluate the design of equipment and systems, chose appropriate materials and products, manage the commissioning process, document certain LEED points, perform the documentation upload to the Green Building Certification Institute (GBCI) for their certification review, and in some cases even complete the design.

There is a significant difference between a LEED-registered building and one that has achieved certification. Firms can say they have worked on a LEED project, even if it has not been constructed. Some might go as far as to say that they completed the LEED projects, because their role ended at design. There are fewer firms that have actually demonstrated their capabilities through the construction of a building and finally to certification by USGBC, as evidenced by the current gap between the amount of registered and certified projects.

The design firms that make statements regarding their green experience based on buildings not yet constructed or certified are not making false claims. A portion of blame falls on USGBC itself through the introduction of the two-phase project submission. As discussed, the two-phase submission process consists of a review of the design-related prerequisites and credit points at the completion of design, followed by a subsequent review of the construction-phase prerequisites and credits at the completion of the project. Upon submission of the design-phase information, a review takes place and results in a conditional approval of the documents. This conditional approval indicates which prerequisites and credits are anticipated or denied. In a sense, the design has been reviewed for compliance with the LEED requirements even before the building is built. This approval is contingent on the project's construction and adherence to the prerequisites or credits reviewed prior to construction. In a project that is being delivered under the design-bid-build methodology, the designer's work is theoretically complete when the contract documents go out for bid.

One of the problems with the two-phase submission process is that it divides the LEED prerequisites and credits into the two separate categories of design and construction. This separation in the process allows a member of the delivery team to complete at least a portion of their work before final submission (at the end of construction). If during the process of construction, something changes and a prerequisite or credit needs to be altered, then this team member often feels he or she should be compensated for the additional work. Each team member may view credits generally categorized as one group's responsibility as alleviating them of any responsibility in achieving those credits. These are the firms that see the project as a group of adversaries instead of a team.

In reality, the conditions of approval are not final until all construction and commissioning activities are complete. The final submission to USGBC/GBCI requires the team to verify that:

- There have been no alterations made to the design.
- Any design elements that may have changed are correctly documented.
- All construction activities were conducted in accordance with the LEED requirements.
- All construction-related prerequisites and credits have been properly documented.
- The documentation has been uploaded to the LEED Online system.
- Payment to USGBC/GBCI has been made for the certification activities.

Upon completion of the final construction phase review process, USGBC/GBCI offers a certification level and, if accepted, the building is certified. The two-phase submission allows the team to submit documentation on some items at the completion of design and the remaining balance of prerequisites and points at the completion of construction. While this methodology is understandable in the context of a Core and Shell building, it is not necessarily supportive of an integrated approach in which the entire team stays with the project. Success cannot be claimed until the final certification is granted by USGBC.

The following is a list of the design and construction related prerequisites and credits under the LEED 2009 for New Construction rating system.

Design Phase Prerequisites and Credits	
SSc1	Site Selection
SSc2	Development Density and Community Connectivity
SSc3	Brownfield Redevelopment
SSc4.1–SSc4.4	Alternative Transportation
SSc5.2	Site Development—Maximize Open Space
SSc6.1 and SSc6.2	Stormwater Design—Quantity and Quality Control
SSc7.2	Heat Island Effect—Roof
SSc8	Light Pollution Reduction
WEp1	Water Use Reduction
WEc1	Water Efficient Landscaping
WEc2	Innovative Wastewater Technologies
WEc3	Water Use Reduction
EAp2	Minimum Energy Performance
EAp3	Fundamental Refrigerant Management
EAc1	Optimize Energy Performance
EAc2	On-Site Renewable Energy
EAc4	Enhanced Refrigerant Management
MRp1	Storage and Collection of Recyclables
IEQp1	Minimum Indoor Air Quality Performance
IEQp2	Environmental Tobacco Smoke (ETS) Control
IEQc1	Outdoor Air Delivery Monitoring
IEQc2	Increased Ventilation
IEQc5	Indoor Chemical and Pollutant Source Control
IEQc6.1 and IEQc6.2	Controllability of Systems
IEQc7.1 and IEQc7.2	Thermal Comfort
IEQc8.1 and IEQc8.2	Daylight and Views
IDc1	Innovation in Design (May be Design or Construction depending on proposed innovation)
RPc1	Regional Priority (May be Design or Construction depending on RP credit selection)

Construction Phase Prerequisites and Credits	
SSp1	Construction Activity Pollution Prevention
SSc5.1	Site Development—Protect or Restore Habitat
SSc7.1	Heat Island Effect—Nonroof
EAp1	Fundamental Commissioning

EAc3	Enhanced Commissioning
EAc5	Measurement and Verification
EAc6	Green Power
MRc1.1–MRc1.2	Building Reuse
MRc2	Construction Waste Management
MRc3	Resource Reuse
MRc4	Recycled Content
MRc5	Regional Materials
MRc6	Rapidly Renewable Materials
MRc7	Certified Wood
IEQc3.1 and IEQc3.2	Construction Indoor Air Quality Management Plan
IEQc4.1–IEQc4.4	Low-Emitting Materials
IDc1	Innovation in Design (May be Design or Construction depending on proposed innovation)
IDc2	LEED Accredited Professional
RPc1	Regional Priority (May be Design or Construction depending on RP credit selection)

Teams quickly adopted the two-phase project submission for a variety of reasons. Certain owners, especially those involved in speculative development, regard early reviews as a way to market their project as achieving LEED certification before construction is started. There are designers who view the two-part project submission as way to limit their responsibility for the achievement of LEED certification. If the design-related credits are reviewed and USGBC/GBCI notifies them that these credits are anticipated, then their work can be perceived as complete and the responsibility of the rest of the documentation process falls to someone else. Typically, this burden falls to the contractor.

Goal versus Achieved

There are many reasons why a team may fail to achieve the goals of a project. A LEED project is no different. However, a team that is inexperienced with the application of LEED strategies will often think they can achieve a credit without knowing firsthand whether it is even feasible.

For example, let's take a project team that includes a green roof early in the design. The team feels that a green roof will contribute greatly towards LEED certification. They believe that a green roof will allow them to capture at least one of the stormwater credits, contribute to the site open space, and help achieve the heat island effect (roof) credit. In addition, they feel that a green roof is synonymous with the definition of a green building. Throughout the design phase, the project team reports to the owner that they are on track to achieve the desired level of certification. They are confident in the contribution of certain credits because they had the green roof in the design. The project renderings reflect the green roof system as a focal point of the design and the owner uses the green roof feature in advertising for the project. After the completion of the conceptual and schematic design phases, the structural engineer is added to the team. As a part of his work, he evaluates the green roof system from a structural viewpoint. The analysis indicates that the building requires additional support to accommodate the weight of the green roof system. The additional support is added to the structural design and the documents are released for bid.

The successful low-bid contractor is asked for a separate estimate for various items and features included in the bid documents. The green roof is included on this list, because while the contract was awarded based on the low bid, the project is still over budget. The team needs to look for a way to be more cost effective and the green roof is a very expensive item. The estimate for the green roof includes the extra structural supports, the green roof system, an irrigation system, and the cost for alterations to the roof manufacturer's warranty. In an effort to save the budget, the green roof is removed from the scope of work. The team still installs a green roof on the portion of the roof that can be seen from inside the building. The result is that only a fraction of the roof is vegetated.

When the team is asked to document the three LEED credits that were seen as achievable based on the green roof, they find out that even if they had the green roof over the entire roof area, the system does not contain enough soil and plant material to significantly alter the stormwater runoff. That credit would have been lost even if the green roof was still in the project. Additionally, the plant mix used in the green roof system is not made up of native or adapted plant species and the site location did not achieve the development density requirement of the first compliance path for achievement of the open space credit. Even if the plant mix was native to the area, it could not be used to satisfy the open space calculations. The end result is that three credits are lost and the team is now looking at a Silver rating instead of Gold. Losing the points is only a part of the owner's issues. The owner paid for extra, unneeded structure to support a full green roof. In addition, the owner has to explain to stakeholders and the public why there is only a small green roof on the completed project.

In this case, the team lacked the experience to understand the requirements of each LEED credit, how the LEED credits are interrelated, and that the choice to include a trendy green product affected the roofing manufacturer's warranty.

THE IMPACT OF PREREQUISITES AND POINTS IN LEED 2009

Project teams that choose to follow a two-phase submission process sometimes assume that once the prerequisites and points have gone through the design review, the work is complete, and the points are guaranteed. As we just discussed, this is not the case. No prerequisite or point is officially awarded by USGBC/GBCI—meaning a project cannot be certified—until the construction of the building and the commissioning of the building systems have been completed. There are prerequisites and credits defined as design submittals that are dependent on the performance of the contractor. Similarly, there are prerequisites and credits defined as construction submittals that depend on the performance of the designers.

Future chapters of this work will address each of the prerequisites and points in greater detail. The following is offered as an overview and provides a few examples of the complexity that LEED requirements can add to a project.

KEY: Design submittals are noted as (D) and Construction Submittals are noted as (C).

SUSTAINABLE SITES

SSp1: Construction Activity Pollution Prevention (C)

This prerequisite is listed as a construction phase submittal. It is the responsibility of the contractor to document compliance to a Construction Activity Pollution Prevention Plan during the construction phase of the project. However, it should also be the responsibility of the design team to furnish a compliant plan to the contractor as a part of the contract documents; this is especially true in the case of a design-bid-build delivery. Because this is a prerequisite, a team must demonstrate compliance in order to be eligible for certification. In a design-bid-build delivery, it should not be the contractor's responsibility to develop site drawings and write a plan that is compliant to both the local codes and LEED requirements.

Stormwater Design (D)

In a design-bid-build delivery, the civil design will be performed by a member of the design team. The corresponding drawings and specifications will be furnished to the contractor. The contractor will use the defined scope of work as the basis of the estimated cost. Contractors may find additional requirements to their scope either in the individual specification sections or in the general conditions sections. These requirements obligate them to apply, pay for and obtain all necessary permits for the project. In some cases, a municipality may not approve innovations that are, at times, applied to achieve the two LEED stormwater credits, SSc6.1: Stormwater Design—Quantity Control and SSc6.2: Stormwater Design—Quality Control. Municipalities unfamiliar with cutting-edge solutions to stormwater management may not be comfortable approving an unconventional design and may require a design change in order to receive the required permits. If the design is modified to be in compliance with applicable permitting requirements, it may fail to achieve the LEED performance standard even though a stormwater plan was submitted during the design submission phase.

WATER EFFICIENCY

WEc1: Water-Efficient Landscaping (D)

The credit points for water-efficient landscaping pertain to reducing potable water used for irrigation by 50 percent (1 point), or using no potable water or having no irrigation (2 points). To achieve these points, the design may call for no permanent irrigation. The contractor structures the estimate in accordance with no irrigation system. However, some municipalities require site irrigation. Furthermore, some municipalities have restrictions on the plant types that can be used in a commercial landscape. A municipality may not allow certain types of native and adaptive vegetation that are used in combination with a no-irrigation strategy. The contractor includes all the components of this strategy in their bid, but is not aware of the municipal requirement. This can result in a failure to obtain permits for construction. In the event they are aware of such restrictions, a contractor might assume that the design team applied for and was awarded a variance from the municipality prior to bid documents being issued. If the contractor does not ask the question during the bidding phase, it will be their responsibility to make the required corrections to obtain the variance and fulfill the requirements of the credit.

WEc3: Water Use Reduction (D)

In LEED 2009, projects are awarded 2 points for a 30 percent reduction in potable water use, 3 points for 35 percent, and 4 points for 40 percent. Water-free urinals use no water and do not require a flush valve or a water connection. These fixtures are a good strategy for teams seeking a reduction in potable water usage; therefore, a design team may incorporate the use of water-free urinals throughout a facility. Unfortunately, if this type of equipment is not allowed by the local municipal code, then it would require a variance to allow its use. Again, the contractor may assume that the design team has acquired the variance because the water-free urinals are listed in the contract documents. If no variance has been obtained, then during the permit application process the water-free urinals would need to be removed from the project scope. This would cause the owner to spend more money for plumbing work not included in the original scope of work. In addition, at least one of the points associated with this credit is lost.

ENERGY AND ATMOSPHERE

EAp1: Fundamental Commissioning of Building Energy Systems (C)

As with Sustainable Sites Prerequisite 1: Construction Activity Pollution Prevention, some commissioning activities fall on the contractor to demonstrate compliance. While the contractor must do most of the documentation, the designers must also be sure to include the commissioning requirements into the construction documents prior to bidding and execution. The requirements of fundamental commissioning will change depending on the size and complexity of the project. The entity known as the Commissioning Authority must be an independent third party separated from the design or construction management team. While this prerequisite is defined as a construction submittal, the contractor may not have the ability to demonstrate compliance. It should also be noted that the contractor and /or their subcontractors may be put into a position where the commissioning authority is directing corrective work. This should be of particular interest to contractors because in most cases the commissioning authority has no contractual relationship with the contractor.

Energy Performance and Renewable Energy

The contractor's role in achieving EAp2: Minimum Energy Performance (D), EAc1: Optimize Energy Performance (D), and EAc2: On-site Renewable Energy (D) is more subtle than the examples provided for the Sustainable Sites or Water Efficiency credits. These energy-related credits can be affected greatly through value engineering activities. During the bidding phase or upon award of a project, contractors are often asked to revisit the estimate and offer "value engineering" ideas to reduce the cost of the project. These exercises result in scope removal and project cost cutting. The equipment, glazing, or other envelope materials might be downgraded to reduce cost. When any component of a green design is changed significantly, all of the related energy credits must be reviewed and validated. An example can be found in moving from an R-19 to an R-12 insulation value in the walls, which might save money but can result in nonconformance to the energy standards used to benchmark the building.

EAc5: Measurement and Verification (C)

This credit, while vitally important to the owner for tracking the actual performance of their building, should not be the responsibility of the contractor. This credit obligates the owner to monitor energy and water use for a prescribed performance period starting after substantial completion of the project (typically no less than 12 months). The building management system must include devices that enable the owner to collect and analyze data on the energy and water consumption of the building. The contractor may be asked to abide by the requirements of the LEED credit even though the equipment and systems were not included in the design. The inclusion of metering equipment and the programming required to consolidate and analyze that data should be a design-related item, not a construction related submittal. In a subsequent chapter, we will further discuss the requirements of this credit.

MATERIALS AND RESOURCES

MR Credits 3 through 7 (C)

MRc3: Materials Reuse, MRc4: Recycled Content, MRc5: Regional Materials, and MRc6: Rapidly Renewable Materials all involve the purchase, delivery, and installation of construction materials. These activities should be the responsibility of the contractor. However, in a competitive bid situation, where the contractor has no responsibility for the design of the project, the selection of the materials should not be the responsibility of the contractor. On a non-LEED project, the competitive bidding process forces contractors to use specified materials to deliver the lowest bid. The contractor is relying on the information contained in the plans and specifications to solicit price quotations from subcontractors and material suppliers. On a LEED project, the competitive bidding process forces the contractor to assume that the design team has investigated all materials contained in the plans and specifications and that any combination of those materials will result in achieving any LEED point sought. However, this is not necessarily the case. The estimator on a LEED project must analyze each material and determine which combination of the specified materials will allow for the achievement of the targeted LEED credits. Some key points to consider:

- Regardless of specific language, the contractor and their subcontractors are expected to furnish financial information to document these points.
- The project specifications place the responsibility of correct material selection on the contractor; it is up to the contractor to decide how much of which material will be used, and in what combination, to achieve any particular credit.
- The contract documents require the contractor to furnish an action plan within a specified amount of days after award of the contract. This action plan delineates what materials will be purchased in order to achieve the thresholds required for each of the material related credits sought for the project.
- Materials included in the specifications may conflict with the performance standards of the LEED protocols.

These requirements force the bidding contractor to look at multiple issues and may not lead to the lowest price.

INDOOR ENVIRONMENTAL QUALITY

IEQc3.1: Construction Indoor Air Quality Management Plan—During Construction (C)

This point requires the contractor to devise a plan that addresses the indoor air quality during construction and calls for the plan to be carried out by the entire construction team during the entire construction phase. The contractor is best suited to carry out a Construction Indoor Air Quality (CIAQ) plan during construction; however, they have little control of the type of equipment specified for the project. For example, if the schedule requires that the permanent air handling equipment be used during construction, then those air handlers must accommodate MERV 8 filters. If the equipment specified cannot accommodate this type of filtration, then the contractor would not be able to rely on the equipment in order to control the interior environment of the project.

IEQc3.2: Construction Indoor Air Quality Management Plan—Before Occupancy (C)

This credit deals with CIAQ post-construction. There are three separate compliance paths that a team can use to document achievement of this credit. The first two involve a building flush-out. A building flush out is the process of introducing a specified quantity of outdoor air into the building after all construction is complete but prior to occupancy. The third compliance option is to have the air quality of the interior of the building tested by a registered industrial hygienist using protocol prescribed by the Environmental Protection Agency. If a contractor chooses the third compliance option, then the corresponding costs are included in their bid price prior to the award of the project. However, in the case of the first two compliance paths (less costly, but schedule dependant), this is not the case. A flush-out requires the correct amount of fresh air to be delivered into the building for an amount of time dependent on the size of the building and capacity of the ventilation equipment. If the required information needed to calculate the amount of time needed for building flush is not included with the construction documents, then it is impossible for the contractor to plan for and schedule these activities. In many cases, the compliance path option for this credit has been left up to the contractor, and information regarding the mechanical system capacity for outdoor air is often absent from the specifications.

Controllability of Systems and Thermal Comfort

As with the energy-related credits mentioned earlier, IEQ credits, such as IEQc6.1: Controllability of Systems—Lighting (D), IEQc6.2: Controllability of Systems—Thermal Comfort (D), and IEQc7.1: Thermal Comfort—Design (D) are susceptible to value engineering. The controls within a green design can be complex. This complexity adds cost to a building management system and typically will require more devices than those in a traditional, nongreen building. It is easy for a contractor to offer a reduction in related equipment and controls because there are plenty of "good buildings" that have been delivered that do not have this level of complexity. However, on a LEED project, these credits depend on advanced operational systems. Deleting these systems in an effort to reduce the overall cost of a project can result in the loss of credits.

CHAPTER 5

Clarify Your Services

LEED REQUIREMENTS

Many specifications include a "LEED Requirements" or "Sustainable Design Requirements" section in the general conditions portion of the specification. These sections often obligate the contractor through broad statements such as "Drawings and general provisions of the Contract, including General and Supplementary Conditions and other Division 01 Specification Sections, apply to this Section." In many specifications, requirements regarding submittals, pay requests, reporting, and project closeout provided in the LEED requirements section were not referenced in the other related documents of the specifications. As a result, the LEED requirements are treated as an add-on or an alternate to a base specification, and the specification writer does not take the time to ensure that the contractual obligation of each section is correlated to the others. More importantly, the information contained in the individual divisions of work does not exactly correspond to the requirements in the general section of the specifications. In this case, the author of the specifications has obligated the contractor by including language such as "Requirements may or may not include reference to LEED" under the heading of related sections. Some green building experts have argued that this clause obligates the contractor to furnish any service required to achieve the owners stated certification level regardless of whether the documents contain specific LEED requirements. This could also be interpreted to mean that a contractor needs to educate himself or herself about the performance-based requirements of LEED. A contractor bidding on a LEED project cannot rely solely on the information contained within the four corners of the specification because, as in the examples above, the product-based specification is layered with performance-based requirements of LEED.

Know the LEED Requirements

A LEED requirement often found in the general conditions of the specifications is for the contractor to create a set of action plans.

As discussed earlier, action plans are written statements of how the contractor will achieve the performance-related LEED prerequisites and credits. These plans require review and approval and can be used as a justification to delay the procurement phase of the project. These action plans also tie directly into another document known as the LEED progress report. A LEED progress report is used to transmit material and cost information for review and approval and is used as a basis of approval or rejection of a pay application.

The contractor's responsibility for LEED is dependent on the contract delivery method and the contract language. Regardless of the requirements or constraints of the contract, a contractor should always attempt to clarify their proposed estimate on any project seeking LEED certification. Many times, especially on a design-bid-build delivery or hard bid situation, exclusions to the proposed bid are not allowed. These cases may require careful phrasing of "inclusions" instead of "exclusions." Clarifications to the contract are important for a LEED project because of explicit and, more importantly, implicit performance requirements. As discussed in the previous chapter, Certain LEED requirements, even those in a design submission, still require review and possible amendment of the documentation (similar to an "as-built") prior to final submission of the project to USGBC/GBCI.

The following examples identify the types of inclusions a contractor may want to consider in a response to a proposal request:

- State the name of the person or entity who will be the LEED specialist for the project.

If the name of the person or firm is not specified in the bidding documents and no question/response has been provided before submittal of the bid, a contractor should indicate this service is by others.

- State the name of the person or entity who will serve as the LEED administrator for the project.

List the services that the individual will perform regarding the LEED submission and the upload of documentation to LEED Online.

- Identify the requested level of certification for the project.

Often a project specification will try to mandate a specific level of certification. In these cases a contractor should take care not to obligate themselves to a level of certification, which can only be determined by the certification body regardless of the services the contractor provides.

- State who the architect and/or the design team will be.

To be more specific, a contractor should take care to clarify that the bid includes only the systems and equipment that have been indicated on the drawings. In the case of EAc5: Measurement and Verification, a contractor can been held responsible for achievement of this credit even though the drawings and control sequence is not provided.

- State the size and scope of the intended project.

Make sure that any LEED services stipulated in the proposal will be applied only to the work associated with the project. Future expansion (office complexes, master plans) shall be addressed in future proposals.

- Indicate the proposed timeline, including design completion as well as construction completion; LEED submission date and desired certification date.
- State who will be the Commissioning Authority (CxA) to satisfy the prerequisite for Fundamental Commissioning.

Ensure that the contractor's role in this effort is clearly defined.

- State whether EAc3: Enhanced Commissioning will be one of the voluntary LEED credit goals.

If so, ensure that the CxA is the same entity providing Fundamental Commissioning services. Again, ensure that the contractor's role in this effort is clearly defined and that a follow-up visit by the CxA will occur approximately 10 months after construction completion. Ensure that the contractor's role in this second visit is clearly defined.

- State the requirements for submitting the project using LEED Online. Is there a two phase submission or one? Who is in charge of administering LEED Online? List the specific credits and prerequisites that the contractor is responsible for.

A contractor may also consider adding the following statements to the response to a proposal request:

- Certification of the project cannot take place until such time as the construction and commissioning activities are complete. The certification of this project shall in no way be construed as the completion of the project stipulate in [clause/section] of the specification.
- Final project submission to USGBC/GBCI is not part of this proposal. The project submission documents will be collected, reviewed, assembled and submitted by [NAME of LEED Project Administrator]. The design team working for the owner will be responsible to generate documents required for the design-related prerequisites and credits called for under the LEED rating system. The LEED Project Administrator, working in conjunction with the design team, will provide a copy of any documentation to the Contractor, if required for LEED purposes, during the construction phase of this project. This action may require written consent from the owner.
- The LEED Project Administrator is responsible for the review of all submittals in regards to LEED compliance prior to submission of those documents to the owner. This action shall in no way conflict with the architectural or design-related review performed as part of the normal course of the delivery of a typical project.
- All contractors working on the project will be responsible for the transmission of the material and/or cost data for all materials purchased for the project. This information will be filed in a central location on the project site with an electronic copy transmitted to the LEED Project Administrator through processes stipulated by the contract documents.
- All contractors working on this project will be responsible for the transmission of all product submittal information called for in the specifications and contract documents. This information will be filed in a central location on the project site with an electronic copy transmitted to the LEED Project Administrator through processes stipulated by the owner.
- The Contractor will be responsible for the collection of all LEED-related documents from the construction team and transmission of these documents to the LEED Project Administrator.
- The LEED Project Administrator will be responsible for the project's submission to the USGBC. Members of the construction team may be required to complete LEED submittal templates in order to document certain credits.
- It will be the LEED Project Administrator's sole responsibility to perform all document uploads to USGBC's web site, LEED Online.

Who Gets the Permits?

A cartoon clipping shows a skeleton sitting on a bench in the waiting area of a county permit office. A young man with an arm full of drawings is sitting next to the skeleton. The caption shows the young man asking the skeleton, "Been waiting long?"

Even when a construction project is not going for LEED certification, the application, review and issuance of a construction permit can take a long time. Depending on the municipality, the amount and level of permit review will vary. Some localities may be a one-stop shop; you make an appointment and all the necessary disciplines review and comment on the drawings at one time. Other jurisdictions may require several sets of drawings sent to various offices at different phases of the construction process, for individual review.

If an owner wants to consolidate expenditures during the project, then it is logical to have the contractor responsible for the permits. In addition, the contractor will interface the most with inspectors throughout the duration of the construction phase. However, in a design-bid-build delivery, it is problematic for the contractor to be responsible for permitting because the contractor:

- Has no responsibility for the design
- Has no input regarding constructability
- Is not asked anything about the budget before a bid request is announced

Despite these complications, the contractor is asked to obtain approval from the local building inspectors, municipal engineers and fire marshals in order for a project to begin. A better system would require the designers to obtain the permits on behalf of the owners that rarely have the staff or the expertise to take responsibility for this activity. The designers spend a considerable amount of time working on the concept plans, details and specifications that will be used to build the project. They have firsthand knowledge of the design decisions. They do not have to interpret the information contained in the contract documents because they created the plans and specifications themselves.

The designer's familiarity with plans and specifications are an especially important consideration as the complexities of the LEED requirements can add time and effort to a typical plan review. This is not the case in all LEED projects; however, if a design team does not have familiarity with the municipal requirements and has little experience with "green" features, the permitting process can be long and frustrating. The general lack of experience dealing with the performance-based standards of a LEED project may lead to complications unanticipated on a non-LEED project.

Instead of the designers, who are the most appropriate members of the delivery team to take the responsibility for acquiring permits to build, the responsibility often falls on the shoulders of the contractor. Special care should be taken when the contractors are required to obtain the permits for a project seeking LEED certification, as the following case study and examples illustrate.

Case Study

The general contractor of a design-bid-build project is required to obtain the permits for a LEED project. The project is a new building abutting an existing building on the owner's central campus. The two structures are to be linked by a pedestrian walkway on two of the four floors. The new building will also rely on some of the existing mechanical equipment (located in the existing building) for the new building. The owner hires an "out of town" design firm for the project. This firm has a license to practice in the local area but has neither a permanent presence in the city nor a working knowledge of the local codes. Additionally, this firm has little experience incorporating the LEED requirements into the design of the building. The contract documents issued during the bidding phase include many green features. Two of these features complicate the permitting process. In an effort to achieve all of the water-related credits, the design team did not include a lawn irrigation system and they included water-free urinals in all of the men's restrooms.

One of the bidding contractors follows the plans and specifications while assembling their estimate. They know it is their responsibility to obtain the permits for the project and they know that there may be issues with these two water-saving features. However, they assume that since they are included in the contract documents, then the design team has received approval from the local municipality already. When they assemble the estimate, they include the water-free urinals but make sure to instruct the plumbing subcontractor not to include the water supply piping that would be required if conventional urinals were being used. In addition, the contractor removes any costs associated with the installation of a site irrigation system. The contractor submits the bid and is successful in winning the job.

When applying for the permit, the contractor finds out that no one in the office has reviewed the project and the two water-saving features (no irrigation and water-free urinals) will require a variance to the code. This particular

(Continued)

municipality requires all new construction to include a lawn irrigation system. Additionally, the city had taken a negative view of water-free urinals in commercial buildings. A variance must be granted by the plumbing board and a special session of the board (with vote) is required before a recommendation will be made and a variance approved. The contractor informs the owner and requests direction on how to proceed. Advised by the design team, the owner instructs the contractor to make the necessary corrections to the work in order to remain compliant with the local codes. The contractor requests additional information: design drawings and fixture selections so that they can work up the price for the required material and the labor to make the corrections. The owner responds, saying that he will not tolerate additional cost for this work because the specifications included with the bid documents state that the work must be in accordance with all federal, state, and local codes. The local contractor should have known the requirements of the local code and should have included the work as part of their bid regardless of the drawings. Furthermore, the owner says that the contractor should have asked for clarification during the bid process, not after award of the contract. The contractor is stuck with spending money for items that were never included in the bid. To make this situation worse, the loss of the three LEED points places the LEED certification level in jeopardy.

In Part II of this book, you will find details on each LEED prerequisite and credit that may be influenced by code issues. Following is an overview of some permit issues that may arise as a result of an uninformed design team or permit review official.

SSp1: Construction Activity Pollution Prevention

Every LEED project must have a Construction Activity Pollution Prevention plan. This plan must abide by the requirements of the EPA regulations or the local laws, whichever is more stringent. On large projects, defined as greater than one acre of land disturbance, the soil and erosion control plan can typically be found in the civil set of the construction drawings. This plan is usually sufficient for permitting and will fulfill the requirements of this LEED prerequisite. In these situations, the civil engineer who produced the drawings has knowledge of the requirements and has included them in the drawing set. However, on a smaller project, the soil and erosion control plan may not be required for permit application or issuance. While the local jurisdiction may not require a plan, the project must still follow the LEED requirement. If the design team follows the requirement of LEED and furnishes a plan when there is no requirement from the municipality, then the reviewers may be confused, slowing the process or even adding permitting costs.

SSp4.3: Alternative Transportation—Low-Emitting and Fuel-Efficient Vehicles

There are three distinct compliance paths to achieve this credit. One requires installation of refueling stations for a specific number of vehicles over an eight-hour period. If a design team incorporates natural gas refueling stations, there may be special permitting and/or licensing required for the owner to dispense this type of fuel.

SSp4.4: Alternative Transportation—Parking Capacity

There are several compliance paths for this credit. The applicable compliance path depends on the construction type and the project's location. The most cost-effective way to achieve this credit is to size the parking capacity not to exceed local zoning. However, a common strategy to achieve this credit is to design the parking elements in conjunction with the heat island effect credit, SSc7.1. In order to achieve SSc7.1, a team must shade, use light-colored paving materials, or use open-grid paving for a minimum of 50 percent of all parking. A designer can reduce the amount of parking to the minimum required by the building's use. The reduction in parking spaces may make it economical to use concrete or another alternative to asphalt. This dual strategy, reduction of paving and use of light-colored materials, can be cost effective and will contribute to two LEED credits. While this solution may be cost neutral when compared to the total required paving, the reduction of total parking spaces below that of local code may require a variance. Variance to the code, while common, can be a long procedure involving many presentations to local planning and zoning committees. These activities can add time to the permitting process and the construction schedule.

SSc6.1: Stormwater Design—Quantity Control and SSc6.2: Stormwater Design—Quality Control

These two credits reward a team for regulating and treating the amount of stormwater that falls on a project site. The team must reduce the total stormwater runoff (SSc6.1) and improve the quality of water through removal of total suspended solids (SSc6.2). Instead of using a typical design by which all stormwater is discharged to the local treatment plant, some of the treatment is done on-site. Many municipalities prefer more conventional solutions when it comes to stormwater design. Without a proven stormwater strategy, the permitting process can be delayed. Rather than supporting innovation, the sewer district can often hinder it. In some cases, extra maintenance may be required, or additional fees may be levied.

SSc7.1: Heat Island Effect—Nonroof

This credit has several compliance paths, one of which is to use open-grid or pervious paving systems in lieu of impervious surfaces for at least 50 percent of the total site hardscape.

A grass paving system is one form of compliance that uses a base of compacted crush stone. A polymer cell system is then placed on top of the base. The cells are filled and covered with topsoil, which allows grass to grow while maintaining the structural load capacity to support a fire truck or other emergency vehicles. While this product can theoretically be used for a fire lane, a fire marshal may be concerned with reviewing a new material and be resistant to allow its use. Often, the local fire marshal will refuse to issue a permit unless conventional construction materials are used for emergency service access. The owner has little choice but to abandon the use of a grass paving system in this situation.

SSc8: Light Pollution Reduction

The project site lighting design must demonstrate that no (or limited) direct light will escape from the project site boundaries. This is typically achieved by reducing the number of site fixtures, incorporating full cut-off fixtures, lowering the height of light poles and placing light fixtures away from property boundaries.

In a suburban setting, most property owners would appreciate that a neighbor is concerned with lowering or eliminating the light that trespasses from their site onto nearby properties. Permit reviewers, however, may see these reductions as unacceptable either because they do not follow the code or they create an unsafe condition for pedestrians or drivers at night.

WEc1: Water-Efficient Landscaping

If a project site requires no permanent irrigation, it is eligible for two LEED credits. The easiest way to demonstrate compliance is not to install a lawn irrigation system. While this requires careful selection of plant species that can grow without regular watering, the lack of irrigation can provide cost savings and a good payback. Many local codes, however, require a site irrigation system and should an owner wish to develop a site without an irrigation system, a variance is required.

Innovative Wastewater Technologies and Water Use Reduction

In addition to water-efficient landscaping, the Water Efficiency category addresses innovative wastewater technologies and the reduction of potable water use. The typical approach to achieving the prerequisite (WEp1: Water Use Reduction) and ten points associated with these credits (WEc2: Innovative Wastewater Technologies and WEc3: Water Use Reduction) is to use fixtures and equipment that reduce water consumption. Designers may select nonstandard fixtures like water-free urinals or composting toilets. While this equipment uses no water for sewage conveyance, many municipalities prohibit them. Contractors may have a very difficult time getting these systems approved. Another strategy for these credits is to incorporate rainwater harvesting or wastewater treatment as a part of the design. This technology may be completely new to a plan reviewer. They may be reluctant to approve this technology if similar systems have never been installed in their jurisdiction.

EAc2: On-Site Renewable Energy

These points are available to owners who employ a form of on-site energy generation including strategies such as solar, wind, biomass and others.

Some zoning codes do not even address these technologies and a plan reviewer may have no guidance for the approval or rejection. Without guidance, it is even unclear as to which department should review the request. This can cause permit delays and unnecessary effort and time by the design team or contractor.

PART II

LEED 2009 and the Contractor

This section of the book details the intent and requirements of each prerequisite and credit that make up the LEED 2009 for New Construction rating system. The impact on a contractor is illustrated through question and answer exercises, examples, and case studies. The provided examples are not the only possible outcome of a LEED project. Rather, these examples are provided as guidance for a contractor faced with the prospect of delivering a LEED project.

CHAPTER 6

Sustainable Sites

Sustainable Sites, 23%

Water Efficiency, 9%

Energy and Atmosphere, 32%

Materials and Resources, 13%

Indoor Environmental Quality, 14%

Innovation and Design Process, 5%

Regional Priority, 4%

Any building development has the potential to be destructive to the local environment. As businesses and communities grow larger and expand into suburbs, the amount of undeveloped land shrinks, placing stress on the natural environment. The Sustainable Sites category of LEED attempts to address these problems by factoring in the natural environment (local geology, hydrology, and microclimate) and the built environment (automobile use, stormwater control, and utility infrastructure) in order to reduce those impacts. The LEED 2009 version of this category grew by 12 points, in order to credit owners and design teams that are willing to lower their environmental footprint by various site strategies.

The majority of credits found in this category have little to no effect on the general contractor, in theory, especially in a design-bid-build delivery method. This is because most of the decisions about where the building will be located are made before the contractor is involved with the project. However, as discussed in the first part of this book, even though a LEED prerequisite or credit is listed as a design submittal, the contractor may be obligated to provide some level of documentation for the final LEED submission and there may be implications on scheduling, estimating, and permitting.

Description	Available	Submittal Phase
Prerequisite 1: Construction Activity Pollution Prevention	Required	Construction
Credit 1: Site Selection	1	Design
Credit 2: Development Density and Community Connectivity	5	Design
Credit 3: Brownfield Redevelopment	1	Design
Credit 4.1: Alternative Transportation—Public Transportation Access	6	Design
Credit 4.2: Alternative Transportation—Bicycle Storage and Changing Rooms	1	Design
Credit 4.3: Alternative Transportation—Low-Emitting and Fuel-Efficient Vehicles	3	Design
Credit 4.4: Alternative Transportation—Parking Capacity	2	Design
Credit 5.1: Site Development—Protect or Restore Habitat	1	Construction
Credit 5.2: Site Development—Maximize Open Space	1	Design
Credit 6.1: Stormwater Design—Quantity Control	1	Design
Credit 6.2: Stormwater Design—Quality Control	1	Design
Credit 7.1: Heat Island Effect—Nonroof	1	Construction
Credit 7.2: Heat Island Effect—Roof	1	Design
Credit 8: Light Pollution Reduction	1	Design
Section Total	**26**	

SSp1: CONSTRUCTION ACTIVITY POLLUTION PREVENTION

Construction Submittal (Required)

Every project must adhere to and achieve this and all other LEED prerequisites in order to attain any level of certification. The intent of this prerequisite is to reduce pollution created during construction activities. The team is required to create a plan that minimizes erosion, sedimentation in waterways, and airborne dust during construction.

Before creating this project specific plan, the team must evaluate the 2003 Environmental Protection Agency (EPA) Construction General Permit requirements and local laws governing this type of site discharge. The LEED requirements require the plan to comply with the regulation that is most stringent. At a minimum, the plan must account for prevention of:

- Soil loss during the construction phase of a project and any stockpiled topsoil.
- Sedimentation from entering storm sewers, streams, and waterways.
- Air pollution with dust or particulate matter.

FIGURE 6.1
Erosion Control Berm

Before a contractor begins to estimate the costs associated with fulfilling this prerequisite, several questions must be addressed. The answers to these questions may have an impact on the price of construction.

Questions to Ask When Assembling the Estimate

- Were local laws compared to the EPA regulations to determine which requirements are the most stringent?

    LEED requires that a plan addressing soil and erosion control be in place for all projects. This plan must adhere to the most stringent of regulations: local codes or EPA guidelines. In the event that the contract documents include a Construction Activity Pollution Prevention Plan, a contractor might assume that the creator of the plan already performed this analysis. However, it is the contractor's responsibility to review the provided information and determine if the plan is compliant with local codes and/or EPA guidelines prior to the commencement of the work.

- If EPA guidelines are more stringent, is the site large enough to require a stormwater permit? Do the plans and specifications include a plan?

    Depending on the size of the project, local permitting agencies involved, and the sophistication of the design team, the contract documents may not include specific compliance requirements for the contractor. Under the current EPA guidelines for stormwater permitting requirements, sites with land disturbance less than one acre are not required to register and apply for a general construction permit. In those cases, the contract documents may not include a soil and erosion control plan. However, in the case of a LEED-registered project, this prerequisite must be fulfilled and a plan must be in place. In the instance where no plan has been provided, a plan must be created before a contractor can price the material and labor required to fulfill the intent of this prerequisite.

When creating the plan, in addition to the inspection, contractors should include maintenance and documentation of the plan as a cost to the project. Again, depending on the local permitting agency this plan may require a set of drawings sealed by a civil engineer.

- Has the civil engineer included inspection forms and reports as a part of the plan?

In the event the civil engineer has not included sample forms for the inspection and maintenance of the control/stabilization measures included in the plan, the contractor must develop these forms. Inspections should be conducted on a regular basis and after any significant weather event. Any and all corrective measures should be recorded at the time of observance and completion of remedial work. While not required by most plans or permitting guidelines, it is a good idea to photo-document these corrective measures.

- Has the civil engineer indicated what control or stabilization measures will be used?

There is a difference between a control and a stabilization measure. A stabilization measure may be a permanent feature of the site design or may be a temporary measure put in place during construction that will require removal and rework before completion. A control measure is almost always a temporary device that will require ongoing maintenance and removal at the completion of the project.

Both stabilization measures and control measures will require some amount of inspection and maintenance. In the case where stabilization is required, careful attention must be paid to activities required during the period of establishment. Measures such as seeding may require watering and mowing, which would not be required for traditional control measures.

- Do the contract documents specify who will be responsible for acquiring the permits?

Depending on the requirements of a contract, the contractor may be responsible to apply for and pay for all permits required for the project.

It is important to remember that the requirements for LEED may be different than those needed for permitting a project. Just because the local governing body has issued a permit for the project does not automatically mean that the project is in compliance with the requirements of the LEED rating system.

- Who is going to perform this work?

   Will the work of the plan be self-performed or completed by a subcontractor? Regardless of the answer, these measures must be in place before land disturbance activities can commence. The project schedule must be reviewed and should include the placement of the stipulated measures.

- Who will maintain the control or stabilization measures?

   Many times a contractor will have the same subcontractor performing the civil and site preparation work do the installation of the stabilization/control measures. In this case, the installation is a part of that subcontractor's scheduled activities. However, the specialty contractor is usually the first on the site and the first to leave the site. If this contractor is no longer on site, who will take responsibility for the ongoing inspection and maintenance of the measures installed? The construction general permit states that the owner and operator of the site are responsible for compliance; typically the general contractor is the "operator" of the site during construction activities. Even if the subcontractor is legally bound to follow compliance measures, general contractors should enforce that adherence.

   When developing a strategy for the execution of the project, these transitional activities must be taken into account. Contractually, there needs to be a delineation of responsibility for this work.

- Is there a stipulated length of time that the control or stabilization measures must be left in place?

   Plans often require control measures to be left in place until permanent landscaping elements have been established and can take the place of the control measures. The design teams on many LEED-registered projects are using native plants that may require a longer period of time for establishment.

   If the plan does not specifically state the duration of the control measures, the estimator needs to ask the question. Vague or open-ended language in the contract can keep a contractor from closing out the project and possibly leave the contractor waiting on final payment.

SSc1: SITE SELECTION

Design Submittal (1 Point)

The intent of this credit is to avoid development of inappropriate sites. The LEED 2009 for New Construction rating system defines an inappropriate site as:

- Prime farmland
- Undeveloped land below 5 feet of the 100-year flood plain
- An area with habitat for a threatened or endangered species
- Within 100 feet of a wetland or defined setbacks
- 50 feet from a water body that can support fish and/or recreation
- Land which, prior to acquisition for the project, was parkland

The LEED rating system awards this point to any project that does not fall within the prohibited criteria listed above.

This is a design submittal, and in most cases the site is chosen in advance of the contractor joining the team. A civil engineer or a responsible party must sign the LEED letter template stating that the project site is not within any of the prohibited areas.

This is an example of a LEED credit that is either in the project design or out; the general contractor has little to no effect on this credit.

SSc2: DEVELOPMENT DENSITY AND COMMUNITY CONNECTIVITY

Design Submittal (5 Points)

The intent of this credit is to award owners who are willing to locate their building in an urban setting. LEED rewards a team with 5 points if the site is supported with existing infrastructure, thus preserving habitat and resources that might be found on a greenfield site. The LEED 2009 for New Construction rating system provides two separate ways in which a team can achieve these points.

The first option is to build on previously developed site in a community with a minimum of 60,000 square feet/acre density. The proposed building and the surrounding, existing buildings must meet the 60,000-square-foot requirement. To document the credit under this option, a team must look at their building to ensure:

Gross Building Area (sq.ft.)/Project site area (acres) $\geq$ 60,000 ft²/acre

Then, they must calculate the Density Radius:

$$\text{Density Radius (lf)} = 3 \times \sqrt{[\text{Site area (acres)} \times 43{,}560 \text{ (sq.ft./acre)}]}$$

to ensure that all buildings within the density radius also conform to the 60,000-square-foot requirement.

The second option is to prove that the building and the site are connected with the community. If a building is located on a previously developed site within 0.5 miles of a dense residential zone (10 units/acre or more) and has pedestrian access to at least 10 basic services, the project can achieve this credit, earning all 5 of the points available. LEED 2009 identifies several examples of basic services that may apply, such as a dry cleaner, day care, place of worship, grocery store, fire station, beauty store, hardware store, medical building, library, senior care center, park, post office, restaurant, and many others.

As with the first credit in the sustainable sites category, the location of a project will most likely be chosen before the contractor becomes involved with the project. In addition, this credit is either in the project design or it is out; the general contractor has little to no effect on this credit.

Even though contractors may not help achieve this credit, they should remain aware of the implications of the site location. Even on a traditional project, a dense or urban location can complicate the construction process because of smaller site areas and the possible presence of unforeseen conditions. On a LEED project, there may be even further use restrictions on an already small site, as is seen in SSc5.1 for protecting and restoring habitat, which sets boundaries for the area of disturbance on previously undeveloped sites.

SSc3: BROWNFIELD REDEVELOPMENT

Design Submittal (1 Point)

This credit awards an owner for locating a building on a defined brownfield site. Under the rating system, this one point is meant for projects in which the development may be complicated by environmental contamination. The LEED 2009 for New Construction rating system provides three means by which a site can be classified as a brownfield. Sites must conform to one of three possible definitions to achieve this credit:

- The site must be documented as contaminated by means of an ASTM (American Society for Testing and Materials) E1903-97 Phase II Environmental Site Assessment.

- The site must be defined as a brownfield by a local, state, or federal agency.
- The building owner must conduct testing of the existing site based on American Society for Testing and Materials (ASTM) standards.

Similar to the first two credits in the Sustainable Sites category, the location of a project will most likely be decided upon long before the contractor becomes involved. If the site has been cleaned up before construction activities commence, then the contractor has nothing to do with achieving this credit. However, a contractor must be careful anytime the scope of work brings them onto a contaminated site. Even though remediation and testing may have taken place, there is no assurance that all of the contamination has been removed. A contractor must be aware and have established protocols in place in the event that contamination is discovered during construction.

ALTERNATIVE TRANSPORTATION

The intent as indicated in the LEED 2009 for New Construction rating system for these four credits is the same: reduce pollution from automobile use and lessen the impact of land development attributed to the accommodation of automobiles. We will not spend time repeating the intent of each one of these credits individually. Similar to the intent, each of these credits allows for award of an extra credit through the innovation and design process category.

SSc4.1: Alternative Transportation—Public Transportation Access

Design Submittal (6 Points)

There are two compliance paths a team can use to achieve this credit. The first is to locate the building within one half mile of existing commuter rail, light rail, or subway. In the event that the rail line is planned but not installed, LEED allows this compliance path if the team can document that the future transit project is funded and the stop will be within the distance stipulated in this credit. The second compliance path is for buildings located within a quarter mile of one or more stops for two or more campus or public bus lines. Any private transit system relied on for obtaining this credit must be usable by all building occupants.

The contractor has little to do with achieving or documenting this credit; either the site is located close to transit access or it is not. The performance of the contractor cannot affect this credit.

SSc4.2: Alternative Transportation—Bicycle Storage and Changing Rooms

Design Submittal (1 Point)

This credit requires a bike rack to be located near the entrance of the building project. The proper amount of bicycle storage is based on 5 percent of peak building users and the rack must be within 200 yards of the entry to the building. The project must also have showers and changing rooms for 0.5 percent of Full-Time Equivalent (FTE) occupants who may want to ride their bikes to work.

This credit requires the team to document that the correct number of bicycle storage spots and proper number of showers with changing rooms are located in the project scope. LEED uses the Full-Time Equivalent (FTE) to calculate this and other credits.

Example

The Full-Time Equivalent (FTE) calculation for a university building can be determined as follows:

FTE Occupants = [total occupant hours (in one day)]/8 (hours in a typical shift)

To calculate FTEs, the occupant type is multiplied by the average number of hours they occupy the building each day. This total number of hours is then divided by eight to derive the full-time equivalent.

Occupant Type	Number	Hours of Occupancy/Day	Total Hours per User Group
Full-Time Staff	10	8	80
Full-Time Faculty	10	6	60
Part-Time Faculty	20	2	40
Student Researchers	30	2	60
Total Occupant Hours per Day:			240

FTE Occupants = [total occupant hours (in one day)]/8 = [240/8] = **30**

The number of Peak Building Users is defined as the FTE occupants plus the number of transient occupants (e.g., students, visitors, customers) present during the facility's peak period.

From the example above, the university building (at its peak period) has a total of 100 students and 20 visitors. Thus,

Peak building users = FTE + (peak transient occupants) = 30 + 100 + 20 = **150**

To comply with SSc4.2: Alternative Transportation, Bicycle Storage, and Changing Rooms, this university building would require bike racks for 5 percent of peak building users (5% × 150 = 7.5 = 8) and showers/changing rooms for 0.5 percent of FTE (0.5% × 30 = 0.15 = 1 shower).

SSc4.3: Alternative Transportation—Low-Emitting and Fuel-Efficient Vehicles

Design Submittal (3 Points)

According to USGBC, low-emitting and fuel-efficient vehicles are Zero Emissions Vehicles (ZEV) or vehicles with a green score of 40 and above. A vehicle green score is given by the American Council for an Energy-Efficient Economy (ACEEE). The LEED 2009 for New Construction rating system also provides a definition of preferred parking. Preferred parking spots are those spaces closest to the building entrance that do not infringe on required handicap parking.

A team seeking to achieve this credit can follow any one of the four options provided in the LEED 2009 for New Construction rating system.

- Option One: Designate 5 percent of the total vehicle parking capacity as preferred parking for low-emitting and fuel-efficient vehicles. This option is the most widely used for LEED-certified projects.
- Option Two: Install alternate-fuel refueling stations for 3 percent of parking capacity.
- Option Three: The owner of the building can choose to provide low-emitting and/or fuel-efficient vehicles for 3 percent of all FTEs. Preferred parking must be designated for these vehicles.
- Option Four: The building owner can create a program for sharing low-emitting or fuel-efficient vehicles. The program must provide for one vehicle per 3 percent of the building's FTE. The vehicles can carry up to 8 people and the contract with the transportation company must be for no less than two years.

The requirements of this credit make evident that the majority of action and decisions involved in achieving these points rest with the owner of the building. The contractor may be affected in a few cases. If the team chooses option two, installation of alternate fuel-refueling stations, this may require special permitting, depending on the type of alternate fuel that will be stored/dispensed on site. The contractor may have to take into account special fire protection for the location where fuel is stored. The refueling stations may require specialty items that impact the schedule.

SSc4.4: Alternative Transportation—Parking Capacity

Design Submittal (2 Points)

LEED establishes three compliance paths for this credit based on the type of building: nonresidential, residential, and mixed use. If the project is located on an existing site, then the team can achieve this credit by providing no new parking.

A nonresidential project can follow one of three options for compliance with this credit:

- Option One: Size the parking capacity not to exceed minimum zoning requirements and provide 5 percent of total parking spaces as preferred parking for carpools.
- Option Two: Projects where the total parking space allotment is less than 5 percent of FTE occupants must provide for 5 percent of total parking for preferred parking for carpools.
- Option Three: This option is only available if the project is nonresidential, and is located on an existing site. In this case a team must demonstrate that no new parking was added to the site.

If the project is a residential building, then there are two options for compliance.

- Option One: Do not exceed local zoning ordinances and allocate space on site for shared vehicle usage, carpool drop-off, and or shuttle service.
- Option Two: If the project is located on an existing site, then the team can achieve this credit by providing no new parking.

There are two options available for a mixed-use type development:

- Option One: If the development has less than 10 percent commercial area, then the team must comply with the residential requirements.
- Option Two: If the development has more than 10 percent commercial space, then the team must comply with the nonresidential compliance options for this portion of the building and residential compliance requirements for the residential section of the development.

SSc5.1: SITE DEVELOPMENT—PROTECT OR RESTORE HABITAT

Construction Submittal (1 Point)

The intent of this credit is to conserve existing natural areas and restore damaged areas by providing habitat, which in turn promotes biodiversity. This credit is accomplished by following one of two compliance paths. The compliance path used by the team to document this credit is dictated by the existing conditions of the site (i.e., greenfield or previously developed).

Compliance Path One—Greenfield Site

In this case, the contractor must confine construction activities to a specific area and restrict the level of site disturbance. The LEED 2009 for New Construction rating system stipulates that the area of disturbance can be no more than:

- 40 feet beyond the building perimeter
- 10 feet past walkways, patios, surface parking and utilities under 12 inches in diameter
- 15 feet beyond primary curbs and main utility branch trenches
- 25 feet beyond constructed areas with permeable surfaces

As you can tell by the allowable area of disturbance, the contractor must have a well-thought-out execution plan to accommodate all of these requirements. If this compliance path is being used to achieve this credit, the contractor must develop a plan early in the preconstruction phase.

Questions to Ask When Assembling the Estimate
- Will soil and erosion control measures be in conflict with this credit?

    The soil and erosion control measures stipulated in the contract documents or called for by the local municipality require installation of control measures outside the limits of disturbance defined in this credit. In this case, this credit may be in direct conflict with state, federal, or local requirements.
- Are the limits of site disturbance indicated on the drawings?

    Most often, the design team has not defined the limits of site disturbance on the contract documents. If there is no indication of these limits included on the contract documents, then a contractor should create a drawing showing the limits before offering to subcontractors for pricing. This compliance path requires strict adherence to site disturbance boundary. If not notified in advance, an unsuspecting subcontractor could jeopardize this credit or be entitled to extra cost during the execution of their work.

- How much parking will be needed for the tradespeople working on site?

    This credit affects construction parking as well as lay-down areas. All site parking and material lay-down areas must be within the defined limits of disturbance.

- Will there be ample room for construction trailers?

    Any disturbance of the existing site is restricted under the first compliance path for this credit to a very limited area. This area must accommodate the location of site trailers, temporary parking lots, material lay-down and staging areas, and any other work associated with the project.

- Will there be room on site for the storage of materials, or will the project require just-in-time delivery?

    Just-in-time delivery can result in the allocation of off-site lay-down or staging areas. These areas can add cost to a project through the requirement of additional security, rentals, drayage, double handling, and logistics management.

- Is there room to bench excavations, including spoils?
- Will shoring be required when bringing utilities into the site?
- Do I have room for spoils or stockpiled topsoil?

    If the contractor is required to bring large utility lines (12 inch or larger) onto the site, they must take into account the depth of the utility. Allowable land disturbance for any utilities greater than 12 inches is restricted to 10 feet. Depending on the depth of the utility, there may not be enough room on the site to set up the equipment, lay down the material, dig the trench, and temporarily land the spoil without going beyond the ten foot limit. Each and every activity that will be executed on the site must be addressed to avoid problems documenting the compliance to these credit requirements. Regardless of how this is addressed in the contract documents, it is advisable to add this requirement to all subcontract agreements.

- Who will photo-document the limits of disturbance and compliance?

    This LEED credit does not require photo-documentation. However, it is one of the best ways to demonstrate that the contractors working on site are abiding by the written plan. It is advised to designate one person on the site staff who will take progress photos on a regular basis throughout the duration of the construction phase.

Compliance Path Two—Previously Developed Sites

This credit is not as limiting for a contractor if the project is located on a previously developed site. Credit compliance is owner-based. The credit requires the site design to restore or protect a minimum of 50 percent of the site (excluding the building footprint) or 20 percent of the total site (including building footprint), whichever is greater, with native or adapted plant species. While the requirement to limit site disturbance is removed under this compliance path, the contractor should be careful when a site requires native or adapted vegetation. Some municipalities will not allow native landscaping due to its natural height. The contractor should ask the following questions:

Questions to Ask When Assembling the Estimate

- Does the municipality allow for native landscaping without a variance to the zoning ordinance?

   Municipalities that have some kind of restriction typically have a "weed ordinance," which restricts the use of plants that are over a certain height unless contained to specific landscaped areas. In order to achieve this credit following the second compliance path, there must be a sizeable section of the site dedicated to native plant species. The requirement of this credit may contradict the local codes.

- Are there specialty contractors in your area that understand and have experience with native plants?

   While there are typically an ample number of landscape contractors in any given area, they may not have experience with native plants. The seeds and plants used to achieve this credit do not always come from the local nursery, and that may entail schedule and procurement issues. In addition to stock availability, the local contractors must understand how to plant and care for these plants up to the point of establishment.

- Are these plants available in your area?

   The native plant industry is a specialty industry. A contractor should not take for granted that this stock will have the same availability as normal turf grass, sod, or ornamental trees and shrubs.

- Does the owner understand what this type of landscape will look like?

   Native plants do not look like a typical "corporate" landscape. A contractor is advised to make the owner aware of what the property will look like once these native plants take hold.

- Does your contract require the landscape to be established prior to completion of the contract terms?

  Native plants are sometimes harder to establish. Many native plants must be planted at a specific time of the year and establishment can take longer than traditional landscaping. The contractor should be careful to stipulate how long they will temporarily maintain the landscape. The contract terms may expire before the plants have time to become established.

- What is the warranty period for this work?

  A contractor should take caution to ensure time limits are set for warranty on landscaping items.

- If the project has no permanent irrigation system, who will be responsible for watering and care until, the plants are established?

  In extreme cases, native landscaping can take nearly three years to establish itself. During this time, continual monitoring and maintenance is required to ensure the seedlings and maturing plants survive, as well as to avoid excessive soil erosion.

Case Study

The owner of this project was fully committed to developing a native landscape. With the exception of any existing trees remaining on site, the team had to utilize 100 percent native plants, trees, and shrubs. The initial landscape designer returned a concept plan that was not 100 percent native in strategy or in reality. The design incorporated non-native turf grasses, non-native specimen trees, flowers and shrubs of all types, noncompliant path lighting, water features (fountain) in the retention pond, and uplighting in select trees. This proposed design would require a permanent irrigation system, extraneous energy use for the fountain, and full-time lawn maintenance to cut the turf grass, and the team would be forced to abandon the SSc8 credit for Light Pollution Reduction. The design included many things the owner did not want. When the owner asked why the designer delivered a design that was so divergent from what was requested, the designer responded that even though the owner wanted an all-native landscape he knew that they would not be happy with the final result. Needless to say, the landscape designer was dismissed from the project team.

(Continued)

Instead, the owner decided to work out a partnership with several private and public groups to find a solution. The owner saw this as a good way to demonstrate commitment to both the environment and the local community. The owner representatives set off immediately to lay the groundwork necessary for the partnership to work. The group formed in no time, and immediately offered solutions and resources for true native landscaping, but some obstacles still stood in the way.

The team had to develop a strategy that would achieve the 100 percent native strategy and be delivered within a small budget. They offered the owner a solution that could accomplish both the size and the budget. However, the plan would require the owner to start the landscape from seed and use much smaller trees and shrubs than what is typically used on a project. The owner agreed.

The native plants proposed could only be planted in the fall and, at the time, the team encountered one of the wettest falls in local history. This set the team behind schedule. There are several native grasses that can be started in early winter, but the winter came so quickly that the ground froze before planting could occur. Though not optimal, the team settled on a spring planting. Unfortunately, the following spring was one of the hottest and driest on record. Many areas of the site would not establish, and the areas that did required a lot of temporary irrigation.

In the end, it took three years before all of the natives were established and the landscape was considered complete. No one on the project team could have predicted that this project would take so long. Fortunately, the owner had a "long view" and was patient with his landscape and team. During the time it took to establish the native plants, temporary measures such as irrigation and erosion and sedimentation control were required. Until the natives were established, the site looked very much like an unkempt weed plot. This drew criticism from staff, family, friends, and the local community. Rather than bend to pressure, the owner extended the partnership and used the period of establishment as a tool for community outreach through classes on native landscapes.

Because of the experimental nature of this portion of the project, the owner chose not to be heavy-handed toward the contractors involved. Contractors associated with the native landscape were paid for their services as completed and compensated accordingly for the maintenance provided during the three years of establishment.

SSc5.2: SITE DEVELOPMENT—MAXIMIZE OPEN SPACE

Design Submittal (1 Point)

This credit promotes biodiversity through dedication of open space. There are three options to achieve this credit. The team chooses an option based on local zoning requirements.

- Option One: This option applies if the municipality has zoning codes and includes a section on open space requirements. To achieve the credit, project teams must reduce the development footprint and/or provide vegetated open space that exceeds the local open space zoning by at least 25 percent.
- Option Two: This option applies to areas with no zoning at all. The site plan must have open space equal to the building footprint area.
- Option Three: This option applies to areas with zoning, but no open space zoning requirements. In this case, a team must document that a minimum of 20 percent of the project site area is left as vegetated open space.

The decision to provide a high ratio of open space on any site is a decision that an owner must make. A contractor will have little influence on achieving this credit. However, the contractor should be familiar with the definition of open space that may affect contractor's scope of work. The LEED 2009 for New Construction rating system allows green roofs and pedestrian-oriented hardscape to contribute to this credit only if SSc2: Development Density and Community Connectivity) is also awarded, and a minimum of 25 percent of the open space is vegetated. Water features and wetlands can contribute as long as their side slope gradients average 1:4 or less and they are vegetated.

Case Study

We recently reviewed a project that included a green roof as a part of the bid drawings. Through the bidding and then preconstruction period of the project the subject of the green roof continually came up in discussions. On one side of the debate was the relatively high cost of the vegetated roof system; on the other side of the debate was the fact that the owner had used this design elements as a focal point of the project ever since early concept design. Faced with substantial budget over runs the owner, as most do, sought every

(Continued)

available cost savings idea. Prior to the final decision to keep or remove this "green feature" from the project, it was discovered that the concept of using a green roof was introduced by the design team as a way to achieve this credit (SSc5.2: Site Development—Maximize Open Space) as well as the credit for stormwater quantity control (SSc6.1: Stormwater Design—Quantity Control). SSc6.1 will be discussed later in this section.

However, once the contractor did her research she found that the project did not qualify for SSc2: Development Density and Community Connectivity. The significance of the site not achieving SSc2 and specifically compliance path 1 is that unless this credit is achieved the team cannot use a green roof as a part of the calculations to document SSc5.2. The contractor also discovered that the proposed green roof system did not absorb enough water to dramatically decrease the quantity of stormwater that would leave the site required by SSc6.1. The owner made the decision to forego the green roof, saving the money that was in the original bid price and this action fortunately had no impact to the overall LEED certification level at the end of the project. It was easy to strike the green roof from the budget: it had been single sourced in the specification and it was essentially a standalone system. The team was not able to save the money attributed to additional structure that was added to the building to accommodate the weight of the green roof system. To realize a savings associated with the roof structure would have required a complete redesign by the structural engineer before the change could be priced. The schedule for the project would not afford the team the time in additional design, so that portion of the project estimate could not be altered.

SSc6.1: STORMWATER DESIGN—QUANTITY CONTROL

Design Submittal (1 Point)

This credit awards designs that limit the disruption of natural site hydrology by reducing impervious cover, managing stormwater runoff and increasing the amount of on-site infiltration. First, a team must survey the existing, or preconstruction, conditions of the site to determine how much of the site is impervious. The amount of impervious surface will determine the amount of discharge allowed from the site and the compliance method that must be used to document the credit. A site that is less than or equal to 50 percent impervious must design the stormwater strategies to have no net increase of stormwater discharge. If the site contains greater than 50 percent impervious cover, then the design must result in a 25 percent decrease of stormwater discharge.

The first option (less than or equal to 50 percent) requires a stormwater management design that prevents the postdevelopment peak discharge runoff rate and quantity from exceeding the predevelopment rate and quantity. This must be calculated using the one- and two-year 24-hour design storms. As an alternative compliance path, teams can create a plan to protect stream channels from excessive erosion and quantity control strategies.

The second option, for sites with greater than 50 percent impervious surfaces requires teams to implement a plan that results in a 25 percent decrease in the rate and quantity of runoff. The calculations must take into account the two-year, 24-hour design storm.

Questions to Ask When Assembling the Estimate

- What technology will be used to slow discharge rates from predevelopment conditions?

    Possible examples include the following:

    o **Pervious paving systems**: These systems allow stormwater to filter through the paving system and then infiltrate under the hard surface into the ground. Pervious paving systems have been proven to help in decreasing stormwater run off quantities. Some questions to ask about this technology include:

    o Do local suppliers furnish this type of material?

        Pervious paving may be in the specification, even if it is not locally available.

    o If the material is available in your local market, is there more than one supplier?

        Pervious paving is still relatively new to the construction market. The availability in any given local market may force a single or proprietary source that could stifle competition and raise the cost of the material.

    o Do local contractors know how to install this type of material?

        Depending on the subsurface conditions a pervious paving system may require a deeper base to accommodate the storage of stormwater. Has this been taken into consideration during the design? The purpose of a pervious paving system is to allow stormwater to pass through the hard surface. If the system is not designed to drain into conventional stormwater outlets or detention systems, the base supporting the hard surface must act as the site detention. This requires accurate design for the depth and composition of the base to allow for the proper amount of storage and ample freeboard as not to compromise the hard surface during freeze and thaw cycles. This type of hydrologic design may require subsurface testing beyond typical geotechnical testing.

- o Does the team intend on using this paving system in an effort to achieve this and other LEED credits?
- o Has the owner been educated on the required maintenance and eventual repair of this system?

  Should the owner use a nonsoluble material for winter protection (sand or cinders), the paving system can become clogged. Once this system becomes clogged it will not function as designed.

- **Open Grid Paving Systems:** Instead of small holes, these systems are made up of open cells. These cells can vary in size from 1 to 4 inches and are usually filled with small aggregate or some type of low growing plant material.

  - o Will the local municipality and emergency responders approve this type of paving system?

    Depending on the size of the opening, these paving systems can make walking difficult. An open grid paving system that has a 4-inch cell can also be difficult to roll a gurney or wheelchair across.

  - o Has the owner been made aware of the conditions of this type of paving?

    As with the complaint from the emergency responders, persons wearing heeled shoes may have difficulty walking across a parking area paved with an open grid system.

  - o Is the contractor responsible for the establishment of any plants that may grow in this paving system?

    Similar to the native grass example provided for SSc5.1: Site Development—Protect or Restore Habitat, a contractor should be careful not to obligate themselves for the performance of the plants in this type of open grid system.

  - o Has the owner been educated on the required maintenance and eventual repair of this system?

    These paving systems are made up of open and closed cells. Special care must be given during snow removal to not unearth or damage the panels.

SSc6.2: STORMWATER DESIGN—QUALITY CONTROL

Design Submittal (1 Point)

For this credit, teams must demonstrate that site stormwater is managed on site before it is discharged, eliminating contaminants along the way. The design must reduce and treat the stormwater that falls onto the site. LEED suggests strategies such as reducing impervious cover, treating through infiltration or storage, and treatment by mechanical means. Regardless of the strategy used, the design must include the entire LEED boundary in the calculations. The plan must treat 90 percent of all site stormwater using EPA's best management practices (BMPs) such that 80 percent of the total suspended solids (TSS) are removed. Both structural and nonstructural solutions may be used.

Case Study

The LEED project boundary is used only for LEED purposes and does not necessarily have to follow the property line. Once the project boundary has been defined, it must be used consistently throughout all of the LEED credits. For this project, the owner purchased a very large tract of land. The legal size of the property was several hundred acres more than the planned development. The project team had little experience with the LEED process and had originally thought that the large area of the site would mean ample space to achieve both of the stormwater-related credits and the open space credits. To follow this plan, the owner had to set aside large tracts of the property to achieve the open space credits, which limited his options for future development. This ill-fated design also made it difficult to achieve stormwater control and treatment over the entire site. The first phase of the owner's development was only focused on a portion of the entire site, and he did not have the budget to install the infrastructure over the entire site. Under the requirement of SSc6.2: Stormwater Design—Quality Control, the design needed to remove 80 percent of the total suspend solids load from 90 percent of all stormwater that falls on the site. This would have required a lot of infrastructure across the site.

Ultimately, the team redrew the LEED boundary based on reasonable criteria; it included all planned parking, the building, the required open space, and the restored habitat area, as well as all roadways leading to and from the site. This action decreased the amount of dedicated open space and habitat restoration and allowed for a single location for retention and treatment of stormwater.

HEAT ISLAND EFFECT

LEED 2009 for New Construction contains two credit points for reducing the heat island effect of a site. A heat island occurs when short wave radiation from the sun is absorbed by large, dark-colored surfaces such as surface parking lots and the roofs of buildings. The absorption of the heat is then released into the atmosphere at a slow rate, resulting in a warmer microclimate. LEED offers two credits for the reduction of heat island. One is for reducing the heat island effect of nonroofed surfaces and the other addresses the roof of the building.

SSc7.1: Heat Island Effect—Nonroof

Construction Submittal (1 Point)

There are two options to achieve this credit. Option one is to address at least 50 percent of the site's hardscape through one or more of the following strategies:

- Shade the area within five years of planting
- Provide shade from structures covered by solar panels that produce energy used to offset nonrenewable resource use
- Provide shade from architectural devices or structures with a Solar Reflectance Index (SRI) of at least twenty-nine
- Pave with material that has a SRI of twenty-nine or more
- Use an open grid paving system that is at least fifty percent pervious

The second option is to place a minimum of 50 percent of the parking under a roof that has an SRI of twenty-nine or more.

Some might wonder why LEED defines this as a construction submittal, because if all of these elements are called out in the specifications and indicated on the drawings, then by means of executing the contract, the site complies. One reason might be that site hardscape is often altered during the value engineering process. Perhaps it is because the landscape/hardscape design is not often finalized until late in the construction phase and is bid as an allowance during the procurement phase of the project. Regardless of the reasons, the contractor must understand what is required to document this point. Areas that will be shaded must be documented using a site plan that highlights all nonroof hardscape. Each of the materials used in the hardscape area must be labeled and a takeoff of the total area must be completed indicating shaded areas and paved areas. Contractors will also have to provide the SRI value of the hard surfaces. If 50 percent of the parking is located under roof, the contractor must document the total number of spaces allocated for the site, what portion of those spaces are covered, and provide product data indicating the SRI of the roof material.

Definition

SRI (Solar Reflective Index) is calculated using ASTM E1980 "Standard Practice for Calculating Solar Reflectance Index of Horizontal and Low-Sloped Opaque Surfaces." It is used to approximate how hot a surface may get when exposed to the sun. Surface temperatures will vary depending on three components: reflectance, emittance, and solar radiation.

SSc7.2: Heat Island Effect-Roof

Design Submittal (1 Point)

Three options are available to achieve this credit:

- Option one requires all roofing material to have a minimum Solar Reflectance Index (SRI). Low slope roofs ($\leq$ 2:12) must have an SRI of at least 78. Steep slope roofs (> 2:12) must have an SRI of at least 29.
- Option two requires at least 50 percent of the roof to have a vegetated roofing system.
- Option three allows for a combination of a high albedo roof and a green roof so that:

(SRI compliant roof area)/0.75 + (vegetated roof area)/0.5] $\geq$ Total Roof area

Even though this is a design submittal, the contractor must provide some documentation. During the procurement phase of the project the contractor will be asked for a LEED submittal indicating the type of material used for the roof and the corresponding SRI value. The SRI can be derived through calculation but it is always easier if this information can be provided by the material manufacturer.

Questions to Ask When Assembling the Estimate
- Will the structure support the green roof?

    Green roof systems increase the weight on top of the roof and will change the amount of structure required to support them.
- Will the installation of the vegetated roof system affect the roof warranty?

FIGURE 6.2
Green Roof Terrace at William A. Kerr Foundation Office, St. Louis, MO

© Debbie Franke Photography, Inc.

- Are there multiple vendors who can supply and install the vegetated roof system specified?
- How will the installation affect the project schedule?
- Who is responsible for establishment of the plants used in the vegetated roof system?
- Will the system require a temporary watering system and, if so, how long will it be required?

 ## SSc8: LIGHT POLLUTION REDUCTION

Design Submittal (1 Point)

The intent of this credit is to minimize light trespass from a building and the site. This effort reduces the building's impact on nocturnal environments by improving nighttime visibility. This credit is defined as a design submittal for good reason. It requires a variety of design disciplines to work toward a common solution. The interior, nonemergency lights that have a direct line of sight to the outside must be set to lower by 50 percent between 11 pm and 5 am. They must also have after hours override switches, either by manual control or occupant-sensing. Light trespass from interior lighting can also be controlled by the use of shields, keeping the direct light off of the glass.

Exterior lighting is also addressed under this credit and necessitates lighting areas only for safety and comfort. All fixtures must comply with allowable lighting power densities provided by ASHRAE Standard 90.1-2007. The site must be classified under one of the IESNA RP-33 zones, such as "low" for primarily residential areas or "high" for projects within major metropolitan areas, and follow the requirements established for that zone.

Questions to Ask When Assembling the Estimate

- Who will provide the calculations to show compliance with ASHRAE and IESNA?

    This credit engages many different members of the design and delivery team:

    - The Electrical Engineer or Lighting Designer must demonstrate that the max candela value of all interior light fixtures intersect opaque wall surfaces. If the max candela value intersects a window, then the person responsible for designing the lighting controls or building management system must demonstrate that these lights will shut off during nonbusiness hours.

    - The Architect or Lighting Designer must document where exterior lighting is located and ensure that there is no uplighting on the building facade or landscape.

    - The Landscape Architect must document the location and type of site lighting so that no light will go beyond the site boundary.

    - The Electrical Engineer must produce a total site photometric drawing indicating where fixtures are located and how much light they emit.

    - The Energy Modeler must ensure that all power consumption for exterior lighting has been added into the energy model.

    - The Energy Modeler, Electrical Engineer or Light Designer must document that the base design abides by both IESNA recommendations and ASHRAE 90.1-2007 standards.

    - The contractor must provide cut sheets on each type of fixture purchased.

- Will the contractor or subcontractor be responsible for the development of the final site photometric drawing indicating credit compliance?

- Because a design review by the GBCI is only conditional, with the final review based on the validation of all elements after the completion of construction, who will be responsible for the final document upload to LEED Online?

A proposing contractor should be careful not to assume responsibility for completing this or any other design phase LEED credit documentation at the close of the construction phase.

At a minimum the contractor will be required to provide a product submittal for each interior and exterior light fixture purchased for the project. They may also have to provide a narrative stating that there was no deviation to the lighting controls and sequence during construction. Additionally, the contractor may be required to provide an "as-built" drawing indicating the placement of all exterior lighting fixtures.

Water Efficiency

Sustainable Sites, 23%

Water Efficiency 9%

Energy and Atmosphere, 32%

Materials and Resources, 13%

Indoor Environmental Quality, 14%

Innovation and Design Process, 5%

Regional Priority, 4%

People in many regions of the world are facing water shortages, and while these shortages may not affect the particular region in which a project is located, it should be every team's responsibility to conserve this resource. The World Bank reports that 80 countries have water shortages that threaten human health and impact the economy. Forty percent of the world—more than 2 billion people—has no access to clean water or proper sanitation. It is unfortunate that most Americans, who live in areas where water is plentiful, squander this precious resource. Equally unfortunate are local codes or customs that force building owners to use more water then they need or want to, as illustrated in the next Case Study.

Description	Available	Submittal Phase
Prerequisite 1: Water Use Reduction	Required	Design
Credit 1: Water Efficient Landscaping	2–4	Design
Credit 2: Innovative Wastewater Technologies	2	Design
Credit 3: Water Use Reduction	2–4	Design
Section Total	10	

Case Study

The owner of a 100,000-square-foot commercial office building set LEED goals early in the project, seeking the highest possible rating for the building. There were two ideas to conserve water usage: a rainwater harvesting system and water-free urinals. The rainwater harvesting system was designed to collect rainwater from the roof and store it in an underground tank. That water would be used as make-up water for the mechanical system and for sewage conveyance from the water closets. The team met with the local building inspector to discuss these two features and to find out if there would be any issues with permitting since they could not find any information regarding these two items in the local building code.

While there was no guidance for or against these design concepts in the building code, the building inspector placed certain conditions on each of these systems. The team was instructed to add two methods of filtration (strainer and sand) plus chlorine treatment to the rainwater harvesting system. In addition, the team had to install water supply lines to each of the urinals even though the water-free urinals do not require any water. Once these conditions were met the permits were issued.

WEp1: WATER USE REDUCTION

Design Submittal (Required)

The intent of this prerequisite is to encourage designers to increase water efficiency through plumbing fixture selection. LEED has established a minimum threshold for compliance at a 20 percent decrease in total water consumed when compared to the calculated baseline.

LEED requires the team to demonstrate water use reduction through a comparison of the design case water usage and a baseline water usage. The calculation for the baseline is established for commercial and/or residential buildings by a usage chart provided in the LEED 2009 for New Construction rating system (indicates how often a typical occupant will use each fixture type) and the flush/flow rates prescribed in the Energy Policy Act of 1992. The design case calculation utilizes the same usage chart for occupants and the manufacturer's product data for water consumption of the selected fixtures. All flush or flow fixtures (water closets, urinals, lavatory faucets, showers, kitchen faucets, and prerinse spray valves) are to be included in the calculations.

This prerequisite has been defined as a design submittal. As long as the design is in compliance with the LEED requirements, the general contractor will have minor involvement with the documentation of this credit. The contractor will be required to submit cut sheets for the fixtures showing the flow rate. This LEED submittal may be in addition to normal product submittals. As with all other prerequisites and credits found in the LEED rating systems, a contractor should clearly state what is in their scope of work. If the contract documents are not clear regarding who is responsible, the contractor may be required (through contract or inference) to perform the document uploads to the LEED Online system.

Questions to Ask When Assembling the Estimate

- Are fixtures or equipment included in the design that might slow or stall the permitting process?
- If there are "specialty" fixtures included in the design, will there be any issues with installation?
- Are the fixtures available in the local market or will they be long lead items?
- Will the maintenance staff require special training on the cleaning and maintenance of the fixtures?

WEc1: WATER EFFICIENT LANDSCAPING

Design Submittal (2–4 Points)

The intent of this credit is to reduce or eliminate potable water used for landscape irrigation. Unlike the prerequisite and other credits in this category, this credit deals with the water used on the outside of the building. There are three ways of achieving points covered by this credit.

- Option 1 (2 points) requires a landscape design that reduces water consumption for irrigation by 50 percent. Teams must provide a comparison of the calculated water needed to keep the landscape healthy during summer needs. USGBC states that any combination of plant species, planting density, irrigation efficiency, captured rainwater, recycled wastewater, or water treated and conveyed by public agency for nonpotable uses can be used to achieve this credit.

- Option 2 (4 points) requires no potable water use for site irrigation. The team must demonstrate compliance with option one and use only captured rainwater, recycled wastewater, recycled graywater, or water treated and conveyed by a public agency for nonpotable uses for site irrigation.
- Option 3 (4 points) requires a landscape design that does not require permanent irrigation. If a team chooses to follow this option, LEED does allow the use of temporary irrigation as long as it will be removed one year after construction.

This credit is a design submittal. As long as the design is in compliance with the LEED requirements, the general contractor will have little to do with the documentation of this credit. As with all other prerequisites and credits found in the LEED rating systems, a contractor should clearly state what is in their scope of work.

Questions to Ask When Assembling the Estimate

- If the landscape design includes native plantings or reduce irrigation strategies, will special permits or code variances be required?
- Will the owner's staff require special training on the maintenance of the landscape or operation of the irrigation equipment?

FIGURE 7.1 Native Prairie at Alberici Headquarters, St. Louis, Missouri

Case Study

In this project, the delivery team understood that the easiest way to achieve the points associated with this credit was to omit an irrigation system in total. The owner understood the issues and endorsed the look of a native landscape. This choice was a departure from other corporate campus settings where one might see lush manicured lawns. A native landscape in this region leans more toward tall and mid-height grasses and wildflowers. At the time of construction there was little expertise for this type of landscape design in the local area, so the owner worked with horticulturalists from the local botanical garden to identify plant species that would thrive in the location without the need for a permanent irrigation. Developing the plan was easy compared to the effort put into convincing the local planning and zoning committee to allow this type of landscape. In order for the owner to install and maintain this type of native landscape required a code variance. The local zoning ordinance has what might be called a "weed" ordinance that prohibits property owners to allow grasses to be more than six inches tall.

Creating the concept and landscape plan resulted in a private-public partnership that lasted long after the project was complete. The scheme that was developed for the site was unique for the area and resulted in reduced maintenance cost in addition to using no municipally supplied water.

WEc2: INNOVATIVE WASTEWATER TECHNOLOGIES

Design Submittal (2 Points)

There are two compliance paths to achieve this credit. The first is to reduce the use of potable water for sewage conveyance by 50 percent. The LEED 2009 for New Construction rating system suggests that this 50 percent reduction can be accomplished through the use of water conserving fixtures or use of non-potable water (rainwater, graywater, on-site or municipally treated) for sewage conveyance.

The intent of the second compliance path is to increase local aquifer recharge by treating sewage on site. In order to achieve the credit, a team must incorporate a system to treat 50 percent of the wastewater generated in the building. Once the water is treated to tertiary standards, the water can be infiltrated into the ground, used for irrigation, or other purposes.

Case Study

A general contractor was selected early in the project planning so that constructability and price estimates could be reviewed through a preconstruction agreement. The contractor also had to acquire the construction permits for the project. The out-of-town design team did not have a good knowledge of the local codes and ordinances. The original design incorporated water-free urinals, but the municipality would not allow these types of fixtures without a variance to the plumbing code. The owners chose not to pursue the variance due to time constraints. The team changed the design to a "low-flow" urinal but ultimately lost the points associated with this credit.

This credit is a design submittal. As long as the design is in compliance with the LEED requirements, the general contractor will have little to do with the documentation of this credit. As with all other prerequisites and credits found in the LEED rating systems, a contractor should clearly state what is in their scope of work.

Questions to Ask When Assembling the Estimate

- Are fixtures or equipment included in the design that might slow or stall the permitting process?
- If there are "specialty" fixtures included in the design, will there be any issues with installation?
- Are the fixtures available in the local market or will they be long lead items?
- Will the maintenance staff require special training on the cleaning and maintenance of the fixtures?

WEc3: WATER USE REDUCTION

Design Submittal (2–4 Points)

The intent of this credit is to reduce the burden on the municipal water supply and local wastewater treatment plants. Teams are awarded points for increasing the water efficiency of fixtures in their building by employing strategies that use less water than a predetermined baseline. The accumulation of points is based on the percentage of water savings beyond the prerequisite of 20 percent: 2 points for a 30 percent reduction, 3 points for a 35 percent reduction, and 4 points for a 40 percent reduction.

As in the case of the prerequisite, a team must calculate the percentage of water use reduction using a comparison of the design case water usage and a baseline water usage. The calculation for the baseline is established for commercial and/or residential buildings by the usage chart provided in the LEED 2009 for New Construction rating system and the flush/flow rates prescribed in the Energy Policy Act of 1992 and further amendments by LEED. This baseline is then used to demonstrate the percentage of water savings in the design case. The design case calculation utilizes the same usage chart for occupants and the manufacturer's product data for water consumption of the selected fixtures. All flush or flow fixtures are to be included in the calculations: (water closets, urinals, lavatory faucets, showers, kitchen faucets, and prerinse spray valves).

Questions to Ask When Assembling the Estimate

- Are fixtures or equipment included in the design that might slow or stall the permitting process?
- If there are "specialty" fixtures included in the design, will there be any issues with installation?
- Are the fixtures available in the local market or will they be long lead items?
- Will the maintenance staff require special training on the cleaning and maintenance of the fixtures?

CHAPTER 8

Energy and Atmosphere

Sustainable Sites, 23%

Water Efficiency, 9%

Energy and Atmosphere, 32%

Materials and Resources, 13%

Indoor Environmental Quality, 14%

Innovation and Design Process, 5%

Regional Priority, 4%

LEED recognizes efforts to improve the building envelope and electrical and mechanical systems in order to conserve energy use, which is predominately derived from nonrenewable sources. As mentioned in earlier sections of this book, USGBC emphasizes energy reductions. If a building uses less electricity, then the CO_2 emissions related to that energy generation are also reduced. In LEED 2009, the Energy and Atmosphere section constitutes 32 percent of all points available, a significant increase in emphasis on energy. The first major change is in the baseline standard used to benchmark energy use in a building. The most current version of LEED uses a default of ANSI/ASHRAE/IESNA 90.1-2007. The second change is through the reallocation of points related to the optimization of systems and the production of on-site renewable energy used in the building.

This section of the rating system is also where an unsuspecting contractor can be saddled with design obligations. Certain credits within this category have been defined by USGBC as construction submittals. While some of the credits within this section of the rating system are listed as construction submittals, they must be incorporated into the design if the contractor is going to assume any responsibility in their achievement.

In situations where a contractor is working on a delivery of a design-build project, the information contained in an energy model cannot be underestimated. An energy model is not required, but is the most widely used validation technique for LEED certified buildings. The model is used to document the prerequisite for minimum energy performance of a building. The information in the model is used to calculate contributions of on-site energy generation, helps guide the measurement and verification protocol, and determines the amount of green power needed for a building. An energy model is more than just load calculations for a building. An energy model will inform an owner what they can expect to pay for utilities as they operate the building in the future. It is highly recommended that the model be done by an independent third party, that the process start as early as possible in the design phase, and that it is used as a design tool rather than documentation for a LEED point.

Contractors delivering a project under a design-bid-build contract must also be cautious of the implications of the Minimum Program Requirements (MPRs) that an owner obligates themselves through registration with LEED. In the event that the building fails to perform as it was intended to, or through systems degradation or faulty operation, a building owner may lose certification. A contractor will certainly be asked about whether the equipment was installed correctly or if the cause of the issue is a warranty item.

Description	Available	Submittal Phase
Prerequisite 1: Fundamental Commissioning of Building Energy Systems	Required	Construction
Prerequisite 2: Minimum Energy Performance	Required	Design
Prerequisite 3: Fundamental Refrigerant Management	Required	Design
Credit 1: Optimize Energy Performance	1–19	Design
Credit 2: On-site Renewable Energy	1–7	Design
Credit 3: Enhanced Commissioning	2	Construction
Credit 4: Enhanced Refrigerant Management	2	Design
Credit 5: Measurement and Verification	3	Construction
Credit 6: Green Power	2	Construction
Section Total	35	

EAp1: FUNDAMENTAL COMMISSIONING OF THE BUILDING ENERGY SYSTEMS

Construction Submittal (Required)

The intent of this prerequisite is to verify that the energy-consuming systems of a building are installed, calibrated, and performing according to owner requirements, and manufacturer's recommendations. USGBC defines this prerequisite as a construction submittal because the activities associated with the commissioning process cannot be completed until the end of construction, and the commissioning process must involve the general contractor and his subcontractors. However, the contractor is not the most appropriate party to document the commissioning process.

USGBC instructs a team to designate a Commissioning Authority (CxA). This person or firm must be able to demonstrate that they have experience in commissioning at least two buildings, and be independent of the design team. However, the CxA can be an employee of a consultant to the design team. The results of their work must be reported directly to the owner. LEED also allows for an employee of the design team to act as the commissioning authority if the building is less than 50,000 square feet. Once the commissioning authority has been identified, they must conduct a review of the Owner's Project Requirements (OPR) and the Basis of Design (BOD).

Commissioning requirements must be integrated into the construction documents and a commissioning plan must be created. This plan verifies the installation and performance (inspection, performance testing, and evaluation of results) of the required systems or equipment. At the conclusion of the commissioning process, the CxA must provide a summary report consisting of an executive summary, history of any problems, test results, and evaluation of the process in total.

There have been many examples where a specification has included the commissioning activities as a contractor obligation. This is far from the intent of the commissioning process but design teams often attempt to push the cost and obligation of the fundamental commissioning into the construction budget. When one considers the requirements of the OPR, BOD, and the integration of the commissioning requirements into the contract documents, it makes little sense to obligate the contractor to these activities.

Questions to Ask When Assembling the Estimate

- Who is responsible for hiring the Commissioning Authority?
- Have the requirements of the commissioning process been clearly stated in the contract documents?
- Will the contractor be required to include commissioning activities in the project Critical Path Method (CPM) schedule?
- Who will be responsible for the management of the commissioning process?
- Who will serve as the record keeper for the commissioning activities?
- If the contractor does not hire the CxA, will there be an issue with taking direction from an entity where the contractor has no privity of contract?
- How much time must be included for the commissioning activities?

- How much time should the subcontractors include for commissioning activities?
- How are disputes handled if the CxA does not accept a piece of equipment?
- Will the commissioning requirements require some equipment to be ordered early or installed out of sequence?
- Will commissioning milestones interfere with other construction schedule activities?

EAp2: MINIMUM ENERGY PERFORMANCE

Design Submittal (Required)

The intent of this prerequisite is to establish a baseline for the minimum level of energy efficiency in any building. The LEED system requires the designers to comply with ANSI/ASHRAE/IESNA 90.1-2007 mandatory provisions or the local code, whichever is more stringent. Teams must take into account the building envelope, HVAC systems, service water heating, lighting, power, and other equipment. The efficiency is normalized by analyzing energy efficiency based on average dollar costs. This is a design-related submission and the contractor has little to do with achievement or documentation of this credit. It is up to the LEED Accredited Professional or a member of the design team to confirm if the default stated in the LEED 2009 for New Construction rating system or local code is more stringent and ensure that the design reflected in the contract documents abides by these requirements.

EAp3: FUNDAMENTAL REFRIGERANT MANAGEMENT

Design Submittal (Required)

The intent of this prerequisite is to protect the ozone through elimination of ozone-depleting refrigerants in all HVAC&R equipment. In a building with all new systems, the contractor will have little to do with the documentation of this design pre-requisite. The contractor will be required to submit a cut sheet for the equipment demonstrating that no CFCs are in the refrigerant charge of the equipment.

If the project is a renovation and if existing equipment with CFC-based refrig-erants is reused, then the contractor may have to be involved. For this situation, a phase-out plan is required, or conversion to a different refrigerant must be made prior to project completion. If phase-out of the old equipment is not possible, the team must employ a third party to explain why system replacement or conversion is not economically feasible. USGBC defines "not economically feasible" as a payback period greater than ten years. Should the third party prove replacement is not feasible, the team must create a plan to reduce leakage of the system to 5 percent and total leakage to 30 percent of remaining refrigerant charge.

Even though this credit is a design submittal, the contractor must submit information about the amount of refrigerant purchased. This submittal may require a separate transmittal to the regular shop drawings required on a non-LEED project. Additionally, an estimator should be clear, either through the RFI process during the bidding phase or through clarifications submitted with the estimate, that calculations required for this or any other credit (specifically EAc4: Enhanced Refrigeration Management) shall be completed by others and is not a part of the contractor's scope of services.

EAc1: OPTIMIZE ENERGY PERFORMANCE

Design Submittal (Up to 19 Points)

The intent of this credit, which awards up to 19 points, is to increase energy efficiency. A building's performance is measured against a baseline. The baseline, established in the prerequisite, is ANSI/ASHRAE/IESNA Standard 90.1-2007 or local code, whichever is more stringent. This credit requires a team to demonstrate the building's level of energy efficiency through one of several techniques.

- Option 1: Create a whole building energy simulation (computer model). The model shows a percentage improvement over ANSI/ASHRAE/IESNA 90.1-2007 based on costs of average energy use and normalized by the local cost of energy.
- Option 2: This option is only available for office buildings under 20,000 square feet. It is a prescriptive compliance path that can be used to capture only four points. A design team must comply with the ASHRAE Advanced Energy Design Guide for the climate zone in which the project is located.
- Option 3: This option is only available for general building types (health care, labs, and warehouses are ineligible) between 20,000 and 100,000 square feet. It is a prescriptive compliance path that awards teams 2 to 5 points. A design team must comply with the Advanced Buildings™ Core Performance™ Guide from the New Buildings Institute.

Points are awarded based on the percentage of energy cost savings over the baseline and are scaled differently for new construction versus existing building renovations:

Minimum Energy Cost Savings		
New	Existing	Points
12%	8%	1
14%	10%	2
16%	12%	3
18%	14%	4
20%	16%	5
22%	18%	6
24%	20%	7
26%	22%	8
28%	24%	9
30%	26%	10
32%	28%	11
34%	30%	12
36%	32%	13
38%	34%	14
40%	36%	15
42%	38%	16
44%	40%	17
46%	42%	18
48%	44%	19

This is a design-related submission and the contractor has little to do with achievement or documentation of this credit. It should be noted that if a contractor is asked to provide ideas to reduce costs, keep in mind that there are many interrelated items that can affect the overall energy efficiency of a building.

Energy Model

A variety of energy modeling programs can be useful or necessary for predicting building energy efficiency and documenting for a LEED submission. In most cases, especially when a project is being delivered using a "hard bid" (design-bid-build) process, the energy model is complete long before the contractor is involved with the project. It is important to remember that all LEED prerequisites and credits must be validated (or amended, if necessary) as a part of the final certification process.

This final check must be performed by someone on the team. For a contractor working under a hard bid lump sum contract, it is easy to assume that same person who modeled during the design phase will validate (and amend) the model before final submission to USGBC/GBCI. When services are not clearly stipulated, interpretation is left to those working on the project. Also remember that in most hard bid deliveries, the architect who is responsible for the design is advising the owner when it comes to the contractor's scope of work. It is unfortunate that the two-phased submission process can be applied in LEED for New Construction projects. As we have mentioned, the conditional acceptance of design-related prerequisites and credits are often seen as acceptance of the work. Once accepted (conditionally or otherwise), many designers feel that their work is complete. Validating the energy model after construction is viewed as an extra service that must be reimbursed.

An energy modeling program can be a powerful design tool if used correctly. Most teams use an energy model in one of two ways. Design teams who are really trying to provide an owner with the "best" sustainable building will use the talents of an energy modeler to help inform and guide the design. They will use the model to test a variety of options, including envelope assemblics, glass selection, lighting layouts, building orientation, and HVAC systems, and in combination with each other to explore the best solution. Once the contractor is brought onto the team, they will compare their best performance with estimated costs for construction and determine a final building design. The other method (and more frequently used) is to use the model as nothing more than documentation of the design necessary for LEED. In this case the design team has approached the project in a traditional way. Sustainable success for these projects is left to luck as opposed to data.

Example 1

After being hired, a contractor is asked to look for ways to reduce the cost. The design includes operable shading devices (louvers) on the south and west elevations of the building. During the estimating phase of the project, the contractor discovers that only one manufacturer makes this system. In order to maintain warranty, the contractor must use one of three "factory-qualified" installers. This limitation comes with a large price tag and the limited choice of qualified installers is going to have an impact on the project schedule. The contractor believes this is a great place to reduce cost. By eliminating the operable shading devices, the estimate is now in line with the owner's original project budget.

The purpose of the shades is to keep direct sunlight from entering the building. Without them, solar heat gain will increase the amount of cooling needed for the building and the energy model will need to be recalculated. The cost savings to remove the louvers, wiring, and controls is $100,000.00. The resulting increase in heat gain requires additional mechanical equipment. This upgrade costs $25,000.00. In addition, changes to the roof structure because of increased equipment curb size costs $7,500.00. Lastly, the building's energy performance had changed by 3 percent. This equates to 100,000 kilowatts of power per year and at 3 cents per kilowatt, the building owner will pay $30,000.00 more in utility bills. The actual savings to the project is $100,000 – ($25,000 + 7,500 + 30,000) = $31,500.00 and that is only for the first year of operation. The owner of the building will pay the added $30,000.00 in utility costs every year the building is in operation. By the end of the third year, this cost reducing strategy will actually cost the owner more money.

Example 2

The electrical contractor makes a cost savings recommendation to use a less expensive light fixture throughout a building. The original fixtures included individual photometric sensors and electronic ballasts to dim the fixture in sunny conditions. The original cost is $200.00 per fixture and there are 300 fixtures in the building, for a total material cost of $60,000.00. The less costly fixture is $125.00 per fixture and has none of the enhancements of the original fixture. The proposed savings is $22,500.00. However, using the same energy cost information from the last example, these new fixtures use more electricity because they have a different type of ballast and they do not adjust lighting levels based on outside conditions. As a result, energy use increases by 0.5 percent, which equates to about $500.00 more per year in energy costs. In this case the energy payback for the original fixtures would be approximately 45 years. Owners will have varying opinions as to an acceptable payback period for their return on investment. However, a period of 45 years would tend to be excessive considering the expected useful life and terms of the warranty on these fixtures.

 EAc2: ON-SITE RENEWABLE ENERGY

Design Submittal (Up to 7 Points)

The intent of this credit is to encourage owners to invest in renewable energy-generating equipment. While it may be good to reduce dependence on fossil fuels, in reality on-site renewables are very expensive. It helps if an owner can obtain financial assistance through grants or incentives that offset some of the cost of equipment.

A building must use on-site renewable energy to offset building energy costs to achieve this credit. Teams can achieve up to 7 points for producing energy as a percentage of the building's annual energy cost. The engineering calculation that supports EAc1 (optimize energy) is used to calculate the renewable contribution percentage:

Building Energy Consumption Generated by Renewables	Points
1%	1
3%	2
5%	3
7%	4
9%	5
11%	6
13%	7

LEED defines the following on-site technologies as renewable: solar, wind, geothermal, low-impact hydroelectric power, biomass, wave, tidal, and solar thermal.

Questions to Ask When Assembling the Estimate

- Do the specialty contractors and suppliers in the local market understand these technologies? Are there any tests or studies required prior to installation?

   Most installations of on-site renewable energy generation require special study prior to purchase and installation. Geothermal systems often require test bores to determine feasibility and the size of the system. Wind studies are frequently required to suitably locate a turbine. In addition, return on investment is usually dependent on the site conditions.

- Is there a warranty, and are maintenance issues covered in a contract?

   Many renewable technologies require unique maintenance, and there may not be adequate service providers in the local area. An estimator should take care to ensure that the terms of the warranty period fulfill the needs of the owner. It is also advisable for the contractor to inform the owner of potential problems, special care instructions, and preventative maintenance requirements.

- Will the supplier document the energy output of the equipment?

   Purchasing and installing the equipment is straightforward, assuming the specification offers sufficient information regarding the equipment. On a LEED project, calculations of the energy production of this equipment is also required. These calculations impact this credit, the 19 available points under EAc1: Optimize Energy Performance and the green power credit (EAc6).

It is important for the estimator to know if the calculations will be the responsibility of the vendor or if the design engineers will perform all of the required calculations to satisfy this credit.

- Who will be responsible for integrating renewable information into the energy model?

An energy model (should this option be chosen) cannot be completed until the on-site renewable energy generation has been calculated and incorporated. The estimator needs to understand who will aggregate the data and complete the LEED templates.

- Are any special permits required for the installation of this equipment?

The answer to this question will depend on a variety of factors: local zoning, type of renewable system, and the physical location of the project. Some examples:

Open source geothermal draws groundwater from an aquifer to provide cooling or heating (depending on the season) and is then returned to the ground. Some states and/or local municipalities prohibit this.

Wind turbines require a tower for the turbine to sit at the proper height and in the proper location to achieve a specific power output. Some local municipalities may have restrictions on height. If the project is located near an airport, special permits may be required from the Federal Aviation Administration. This information is critical if the contract documents require the contractor to obtain the permits.

- Is any special equipment required by the local utility?

Many owners have intentions to sell surplus power generated by their renewable energy systems back to the local utility provider. While many local utility companies welcome this, in most cases the local utility provider will require special preventative equipment to protect the grid. It is a very dangerous situation to have energy "back feed" into the grid during an outage. This equipment can be very expensive and is seldom included with the generation equipment purchased for the project unless specifically called for in the specifications.

- If working on a union project, will there be any disruption to the work due to jurisdiction?

EAc3: ENHANCED COMMISSIONING

Construction Submittal (2 points)

This credit expands the responsibilities outlined in the prerequisite for Fundamental Commissioning (EAp1). The CxA must become involved early in the design phase and execute additional activities after systems performance verification has been completed. LEED defines this credit as a construction submittal most likely because Enhanced Commissioning is not completed until all construction activities are finalized and a follow-up review has been conducted approximately ten months after substantial completion of the project.

Unlike the prerequisite, this credit requires the commissioning authority to be an independent third party not connected to the design or construction management team. The process begins before the construction document phase of design. At a minimum, the commissioning authority must perform one commissioning design review. This review consists of the Owner's Project Requirements (OPR), Basis of Design (BOD), and design documents. Early in the construction procurement phase, the commissioning authority reviews the contractor's submittals for items being commissioned. The commissioning authority also requests the operation and maintenance manuals for all equipment. This information is compiled into a systems manual for the owner's operating staff.

During the construction phase of the project, the commissioning authority performs the activities that are detailed in the prerequisite explained at the beginning of this section. Near the completion of the construction phase, the commissioning authority ensures that owner and occupant training is completed. Approximately ten months after substantial completion of the project, the commissioning authority returns to the building and reviews the building operation with the facilities staff and the building occupants.

Questions to Ask When Assembling the Estimate

- Has the commissioning authority been selected?
- Has the CxA completed a design review? If not, can the review change the scope of work?
- Who will be responsible for maintaining the issues log?
- Who will be responsible for keeping minutes from the commissioning meetings?
- Will the contractor be responsible for the CxA services?

    While it is very unlikely that the contractor would be asked to include enhanced commissioning services in the bid, this has occurred. In this case, the contractor must know the scope of commissioning. Depending on the level of detail and the size and complexity of the project, this request may add a full-time person to the site management team.

- Will the CxA be directing the work of the contractor(s)?

    Every commissioning authority performs their services a little differently. This is based on their experience and on the specific project. A commissioning authority may ask for items/activities that are not included in the contract documents. Even though the Commissioning Authority is acting as the owner's agent, they may not have the authority to authorize additional work. A contractor should clarify who can and cannot direct work, and the process for change orders and payment for new services.

- Will the contractor have to furnish workspace (desk, phone, fax, etc.) on-site for the CxA?

    On a smaller project, the commissioning authority will not spend considerable amounts of time on-site. On large, complex projects, however, the commissioning activities may require multiple agents and may require a full time staff provided by the commissioning authority. If an estimate is being assembled for a large project, find out how the commissioning process will work and what support services will be expected.

- When will the warranty period of the commissioned equipment begin?

    On a LEED project, the equipment must be reviewed and inspected prior to that equipment being used for any reason. In other words, if the construction schedule requires the HVAC equipment to be used for indoor environmental stabilization during construction, it must be commissioned before that use. If the installing contractor has participated in the commissioning of that equipment, they may view the finalization of that process as the start of warranty. Depending on the length of the project, this may require the contractor to purchase extended warranties for select pieces of equipment to remain contract compliant at the period of substantial completion.

- Will the contractor have to schedule additional training to satisfy the requirements defined by the CxA?

    Enhanced commissioning requires the commissioning authority to review, witness, and confirm that the amount of training provided to the owner's staff is sufficient to allow those individuals to operate the building. In most cases, the contractor must furnish additional training, including (possibly) off-site training, multiple visits by a manufacturer's representative, or video recording of the training classes.

- Will the shop drawing review take longer due to additional equipment review by the CxA?

    The commissioning authority must review all shop drawings related to the equipment/systems that will be commissioned. This is an additional step, not encountered on a non-LEED project. The contractor must find out if this additional review will add time to the response cycle. In most cases, the information reviewed by the CxA is for equipment that has long lead times and could have schedule implications.

- Has a commissioning schedule been included in the bid documents?

    The commissioning process requires a systematic review, inspection, and conditional acceptance of the equipment and systems found in a LEED building. This process affects the contractor's ability to schedule, install, and turn on select pieces of equipment during the construction process. The commissioning schedule (if provided during estimating) must be reviewed to determine if the stated commissioning activities coincide with the overall construction schedule. If no commissioning schedule is included in the bidding documents, then the delivery team must remember to account for the time of the commissioning activities when assembling the overall project delivery schedule, including shop drawing reviews, prefunctional/functional inspections, testing/demonstration of equipment operation, and training of the owner's staff.

- Who will be responsible for updating the commissioning schedule?

- Will the commissioning schedule be integrated into the construction schedule?

- Are the subcontractors aware that equipment manuals must be furnished early?

    Part of the services of enhanced commissioning includes the creation of an "Operations Manual" which is in addition to the owner's manuals usually supplied with the equipment. This manual is created by the commissioning authority and is an assembly of all of the manufacturer's information, sequence of operations and recommendations by the CxA for the facility management staff. Because the CxA must complete this document before training begins, a request for operation and maintenance manuals ("O&M's") will be made much earlier than on a non-LEED project. All contractors furnishing commissioned equipment should be aware of this requirement, and the contractor should account for this activity on the submittal log.

- Will the contractor have to return to the building ten months after substantial completion to assist in the follow-up commissioning process?

    If an owner wants the contractor to assist the commissioning authority for this ten-month review, then there will be costs associated with keeping the project open and possible remobilization efforts. However, if an owner is willing to pay for the contractor to return during the final commissioning process for this credit, it is a way for the contractor to perform their own review of construction-related items. A contractor may choose to view this as an opportunity to review the completed work and address the client's satisfaction. If a problem is discovered within the commissioned systems or elsewhere, the contractor has an opportunity to correct those items before a service call is triggered. Solving a problem before a service call can sometimes save money.

- Will the commissioning process effect the definition of project completion?

    This is an important but often overlooked question. The enhanced commissioning process is complete when the CxA returns to the site and performs a functional check of the equipment approximately ten months after substantial completion and occupancy. Most specifications do not include language covering this activity. As is the case with most items of a contract, if it is not specifically called out it may be included by inference. A contractor should be clear, either through a clarification or an exclusion, as to the amount of obligation this LEED credit may add to the contract.

EAc4: ENHANCED REFRIGERANT MANAGEMENT

Design Submittal (2 Points)

The intent of this credit is to reduce environmental ozone depletion and global warming potential through refrigerant selection.

    There are two compliance paths a team can choose to accomplish this credit. The first option is not to use any refrigerants (or natural refrigerants such as ammonia) in the HVAC&R equipment. The second option is to select refrigerants that minimize or eliminate ozone depletion and global warming potential. LEED defines the effect based on the refrigerant's lifecycle ozone depletion potential (LCODP) and its lifecycle global warming potential (LCGWP). To qualify for this credit, the project's HVAC&R equipment must comply with the calculation: $LCGWP + LCODP \times 10^5$ is less than or equal to 100. This calculation must be used for the sum of all the mechanical units. Small HVAC units (those containing under 0.5 lbs of refrigerant) do not have to be included in the calculation. In addition, there cannot be any ozone-depleting substances in the fire suppression systems regardless of the option the team follows. This is a design-related submittal, but a contractor will have to submit information (a cut sheet or other manufacturer data) that indicates the type of refrigerant used to charge the HVAC&R equipment.

Questions to Ask When Assembling the Estimate

- Who is going to complete the calculations for this credit?

    Even though this credit is listed as a design submission, contractors may be asked to complete the calculations.

- Do the contract documents reflect the LEED requirements?

    In other words, is the equipment compliant with this credit? Design teams may specify a piece of equipment without performing the calculations needed to document compliance. It is not only about the type of refrigerant used, but also the amount. A system may be specified with a "compliant" type of refrigerant, but if the quantity of that refrigerant is too large then it will not comply with this credit.

- Will a potential value engineering suggestion change the outcome of this calculation?

    The mechanical equipment can be a starting point during cost-cutting exercises. Contractors should be cautious when suggesting equipment changes because this may affect this credit as well as other energy and/or indoor environmental quality credits. If this is requested by an owner, the contractor should always ask that a change be reviewed by the mechanical engineer for LEED compliance before a final decision is made.

Definitions

Lifecycle: The sum of all raw material production, manufacture, distribution, use, and disposal including all intervening transportation steps necessary or caused by a product is the life cycle of the product.

Ozone Depletion Potential (ODP): A number that refers to the amount of ozone depletion caused by a substance. The ODP is the ratio of the impact on ozone of a chemical compared to the impact of a similar mass of CFC-11. Thus, the ODP of CFC-11 is defined to be 1.0. Other CFCs and HCFCs have ODPs ranging from 0.01 to 1.0. Halons have ODPs that range up to 10. Carbon tetrachloride has an ODP of 1.2, and the ODP of methyl chloroform is 0.11. HFCs have zero ODP because they do not contain chlorine.

Global Warming Potential (GWP): An index describing the radiative characteristics of well-mixed greenhouse gases that represents the combined effect of the differing times these gases remain in the atmosphere and their relative effectiveness in absorbing outgoing infrared radiation. This index approximates the time-integrated warming effect of a unit mass of a given greenhouse gas in the atmosphere, relative to that of CO_2.

EAc5: MEASUREMENT AND VERIFICATION

Construction Submittal (3 Points)

The intent of this credit is to provide information about building energy consumption over time. In addition, USGBC now requires the owner to collect energy and water consumption data through the Minimum Program Requirements (MPRs). An owner has three compliance methods for this USGBC requirement and two of those compliance paths allow achievement of this credit. In order to satisfy this credit, a team must develop and implement a Measurement and Verification (M&V) plan. The plan must be in accordance with International Performance Measurement and Verification Protocol (IPMVP), and the owner must commit to following the M&V plan for at least one year of post-construction occupancy. The IPMVP offers several methods for building measurement and LEED defines the acceptable options.

IPMVP Option B (Energy Conservation Measures or ECM) uses data capture to determine savings on defined building components. This option is typically for smaller, simpler buildings. IPMVP Option D (savings determined at the whole-building level) requires building and systems energy use to be measured. This requires data collection at the main meters and may include submeters to compare the actual energy usage with the energy consumption defined in the energy model used for the EAc1: Optimize Energy Performance, explained earlier in this section.

This credit is a construction submittal, but depending on building size and complexity, this credit often requires coordination between the electrical, mechanical, and building controls designers. A system may require specific equipment such as meters, submeters, or data loggers to collect and store the data needed to measure and verify the performance of a building. This should be built into the design before the contractor is involved. Once the systems information is collected, the operator receives a written protocol describing how to use and interpret the data and compare it to the energy model. If on-site renewables are used in the project (EAc2), this equipment must also be metered. All of this detailed information is compared to the results of the energy model and displayed in such a way that the information is useful to the owner or building operator.

Questions to Ask When Assembling the Estimate

- Do the contractor and the subcontractors understand the requirement of this credit?

    There are two distinct parts to this credit. First, equipment must be included in the project design to make data available. Second, a protocol must be written for the owner to compare modeled performance with actual performance of building systems.

- Have the LEED requirements been integrated into the bid documents?

    On a hard bid project, it is the responsibility of the designers to include the equipment or management systems needed within the contract documents. Additionally, someone must take responsibility to write the protocol that will be used by the owner after the construction is complete. This credit is listed as a construction submission, but the designers are better positioned to write the plan.

- Who is responsible for creating the measurement and verification plan?

  As stated in the answer above, a protocol or plan is required to satisfy this credit, and the designers are best suited to write this plan. However, often this plan is not included in the contract documents. During the estimating phase of a project, the contractor should ask if this plan exists. If it does not, the contractor should include the cost of creating this plan in their bid as an alternate, or include language that specifically excludes this from the scope.

- Are the results of the energy model included in the bid documents?

  The M&V plan must include a method for the building owner to compare modeled energy use with actual energy use. If the contractor assumes the responsibility to create this plan, then the energy model must be provided to complete the plan and satisfy the requirements of this credit.

- Who is responsible for documenting this credit?

- Who is responsible for the upload to LEED Online?

Case Study

A design-bid-build project does not include the controls required to achieve this credit in the contract documents. The contractor has no LEED experience and does not realize this, nor do they have the expertise to write such a plan. The contractor simply assumes that the designers of the building have taken care of this credit. At the beginning of the project, the contractor is asked to submit their LEED action plan indicating how this credit is to be achieved and the contractor is forced to hire someone to develop this plan. The consultant who reviews the contract documents informs the owner that the equipment and systems required for this credit are not incorporated into the design. Because this is a construction submittal, the design team is hesitant to take responsibility for this omission.

In a straightforward design-bid-build project, the contractor is only obligated to items identified and included in the bid documents. On this project, the LEED requirements added into the specifications are not truly integrated. This lack of integration blends the product specifications with the performance requirements of LEED. Fortunately for the contractor, the owner has enough experience to obligate the design team to complete the design so that the contractor can price the required equipment.

EAc6: GREEN POWER

Construction Submittal (2 Points)

The intent of this credit is to encourage development of grid-source renewable energy technologies. Keep in mind that part of USGBC's mission is to transform the market-place. If more consumers purchase grid source renewable energy, more carbon-free energy will be produced. In order to achieve this credit, an owner must provide at least 35 percent of the building's required electricity from renewable sources generated off-site. The purchase agreement for the green power must be for at least two years. The building electrical consumption is determined by the energy model created to document EAc1: Optimize Energy Performance. If a team pursues a different compli-ance path for EAc1 and does not create an energy model, LEED instructs the team to use the Department of Energy's (DOE) Commercial Buildings Energy Consumption Survey (CBECS) to determine the project's estimated energy needs.

There are several ways to achieve this credit. The green power source can include solar, wind, geothermal, biomass, and low impact hydroelectric. If the building is located in an open electrical market, the team must purchase from a Green-e certified provider. If a building is located in a closed electrical market, then the owner must use a Green-e accredited utility program. If a Green-e certified provider/utility is not available, the owner can purchase Renewable Energy Credits (RECs). In addition, the vendor does not have to be Green-e certified as long as they can demonstrate that they meet the same criteria of certified vendors and be verified by a third party.

This credit is a construction submittal even though the owner must ultimately decide to participate. This credit can be pursued at any time during the project and does not have any effect on other credits. The only reason this is a construction submittal is because there may be adjustments to the energy model due to value engineering or change orders. Remember that the energy model is used to determine how much electricity constitutes 35 percent of the building's consumption.

Questions to Ask When Assembling the Estimate

- Is this credit a goal for your project?
- Do the contract documents clearly state who will purchase the green power?

Because this is a construction submittal, the estimator working on the project should know how this credit will be obtained. Anyone working on the project delivery team can purchase RECs; however, if this will be the contractor's responsibility, they must know how much money to budget for purchase at a later date.

- If the contractor is to fulfill the requirements of the credit, has an energy model been provided?

There are two ways to obtain the cost for this credit. The first is to use the information generated from the energy model produced to satisfy the requirements of EAc1: Optimize Energy Performance. The second is to use the information provided in the DOE's CBECS database.

- If the contract documents call for agreement with the local utility provider, does the two-year requirement for this credit affect the terms your warranty?

Any time there is a discussion of extending past a normal warranty period, a contractor should take care to clearly define their obligation to the owner. A requirement to purchase the RECs is a relatively easy thing, but if the owner wants to extend a contractor's obligation to a project through extended service or warranty periods, the cost associated with those expanded services should be borne by the owner.

CHAPTER 9

Materials and Resources

Sustainable Sites,
23%

Water Efficiency,
9%

Energy and
Atmosphere, 32%

Materials and
Resources, 13%

Indoor
Environmental
Quality, 14%

Innovation and
Design Process,
5%

Regional Priority,
4%

The Materials and Resources section of the LEED rating system affects a contractor more than any other LEED section. While Materials and Resources constitutes only 13 percent of the point total, all credits in this section, except for the prerequisite, are the responsibility of the contractor. The contractor has the responsibility to plan, procure, demonstrate, document, and submit evidence to support these credits during the LEED certification process.

The credit documentation in this section requires the estimator to make some critical decisions. On a non-LEED, hard-bid project, the estimate is based on the information contained in the contract documents. The estimator performs a quantity survey, and then matches it with cost based on the lowest priced material as prescribed by the specifications. Once the estimate is complete the bid is offered, and upon notification of award, the contractor prepares the product and material submittals to begin procurement. The approved products are delivered to the project site and installed. On a project seeking LEED certification, all of these elements—preconstruction, project planning, procurement, subcontractor buyout, and contractual issues—are completed in the same fashion. The difference is that on a LEED project, the product specification is overlaid with the performance requirements of the LEED rating system. On a LEED project, the product specification becomes a performance base specification. Before a final decision on material choice can be made, the contractor must assess each product and see how they are coordinated with all other materials to ensure that the material credits are achievable.

Most contractors believe that if an item is not in the contract, then it is not in their scope. For LEED, a contractor must know the requirements of the LEED standard to determine if the contract documents clearly state what must be provided. We will provide specific examples on a point-by-point basis later in this chapter. One example is that for LEED projects, extra requirements are included in the general section of the specification under "LEED or Sustainable Requirements." In this section the contractor is directed to create an action plan demonstrating how they will achieve certain points indicated on the LEED score card. In a straightforward non-LEED project, the contractor bases the low bid on materials included in the specific sections of the specifications. On a LEED project, the contractor must run through multiple pricing exercises to see what combinations of materials included in the specification will result in complying with the LEED credits included in the specification. Some might argue that this is not the contractor's responsibility, especially in a design-bid-build contract. One might also trust that the specification writer has cross-checked all the products listed in the specification to meet the LEED criteria. Unfortunately, this is rarely the case. Often specifications may be recycled from other projects. Items, language, and products get carried over from unrelated projects and are missed during final review before the documents are issued for construction or bid. Additionally, the casual addition of LEED language into a specification without complete integration creates vague and implied responsibilities that could fall to multiple parties in a contract.

Description	Available	Submittal Phase
Prerequisite 1: Storage and Collection of Recyclables	Required	Design
Credit 1.1: Building Reuse—Maintain Existing Walls, Floors, and Roof	1–3	Construction
Credit 1.2: Building Reuse—Maintain Interior Nonstructural Elements	1	Construction
Credit 2: Construction Waste Management	1–2	Construction
Credit 3: Materials Reuse	1–2	Construction
Credit 4: Recycled Content	1–2	Construction
Credit 5: Regional Materials	1–2	Construction
Credit 6: Rapidly Renewable Materials	1	Construction
Credit 7: Certified Wood	1	Construction
Section Total	**14**	

The material credits are defined by ratios. Some examples include the ratio of reused building components (those that stay in place) to preconstruction components (MRc1: Building Reuse), the ratio of construction and demolition waste diverted from the landfill to the total amount of waste generated on the site (MRc2: Construction Waste Management), and the ratio of reused material in the project to the new material purchased (MRc3: Materials Reuse).

MRp1: STORAGE AND COLLECTION OF RECYCLABLES

Design Submittal (Required)

The intent of this prerequisite is to recycle materials in the building after the owner takes occupancy of the space. The design team must include areas in the building that are easily accessible and dedicated to recycling of materials. The owner must, at a minimum, recycle paper, cardboard, glass, plastics, and metals.

This is a design-related LEED submittal and responsibility for compliance falls to the design team. The team must submit drawings highlighting the collection areas, a statement from the owner with their commitment to recycle, and a list of the materials to be recycled. As long as the contractor builds what is indicated on the drawings, there are no additional responsibilities for this prerequisite. It is the obligation of the building owner/operator to support the recycling plan after construction is complete.

BUILDING REUSE

Construction Submittal (Up to 4 Points)

The building reuse credits reward a team for reusing parts of an existing building and are considered construction submittals. MRc1.1: Building Reuse—Maintain Existing Walls, Floors, and Roof is worth up to 3 points depending on the percentage of existing building structure and envelope is maintained (55 percent retention is awarded 1 point, 75 percent is awarded 2 points and 95 percent is awarded 3 points). Windows and nonstructural roof are excluded from the calculations. MRc1.2: Building Reuse—Maintain Interior Nonstructural Elements awards 1 point for the reuse of existing interior nonstructural features, such as doors, ceiling systems, and interior walls for at least 50 percent of the total area of interior nonstructural elements. LEED recognizes an owner who chooses to extend the lifecycle of existing building stock instead of building a brand new building. Building reuse conserves material and cultural resources as well as reduces waste and the environmental impacts caused by new construction.

To comply with these credits, the contractor must quantify the reused elements (separated into structural and nonstructural materials) by surface area. The structural elements saved are compared to the preexisting condition and the nonstructural elements are compared with total nonstructural elements after construction is complete.

If the project is a combination of an existing building and an addition/new construction, then the new construction cannot be more than twice the size of the existing structure. If it is, this credit is not applicable. In this case, teams can apply the structure saved to calculations for credit MRc2: Construction Waste Management instead. Keep in mind that the materials can only be counted once and must not appear in both MRc1 and MRc2 credits.

Questions to Ask When Assembling the Estimate

- Have all of the elements to remain in the existing structure been identified on the drawings?
- Have the remaining items been inspected and are they free of hazardous materials?
- Will any temporary bracing or shoring be needed? If so, who will be responsible for the engineering?
- Who will be responsible for completing the LEED documentation?
- Who will perform the calculations after selective demolition?
- Has a structural investigation been completed prior to the start of selective demolition?
- Will there be any special considerations when connecting to existing assemblies?
- Do the contract documents protect the contractor from failure of reused materials?

MRc2: CONSTRUCTION WASTE MANAGEMENT

Construction Submittal (Up to 2 Points)

The intent of this credit is to divert construction and demolition debris from landfills or incinerators. It encourages redirecting recyclable resources back to the manufacturing processes and redirecting reusable materials to appropriate projects.

The credit requires the contractor to recycle or salvage at least 50 percent (1 point) and 75 percent (2 points) of all construction and demolition waste. As with previous credits, hazardous waste is not included in calculations for this credit. Additionally, debris generated by land clearing activities (including excavation) are not included in this calculation. A Construction Waste Management (CWM) plan must be developed and include:

- A list of all materials the team plans to divert during construction or demolition.
- A plan of how the materials will be collected: either sorted on-site, or off site.
- How the waste will be quantified: either by weight or volume. The choice is up to the team but the measurement must be consistent throughout the entire project.
- A list of items that may be donated or salvaged (on-site or off).

The CWM plan must be established prior to mobilization on-site. Once the plan has been developed, reviewed, and approved, the contractor will need to document the construction recycling progress on a monthly basis. This documentation should include:

- Construction waste tables as identified on the LEED submittal templates.
- The type of waste generated and the company hauling the materials.
- The drop-off location for the waste or recycled materials.
- The amount of waste on each haul (weight or volume).

As mentioned in Building Reuse, if the project includes building reuse/renovation but the retained amounts will not qualify for the MRc1.1 or MRc1.2, the material can be applied to this credit.

Questions to Ask When Assembling the Estimate
- Are there local recycling centers that will accept construction and demolition waste?
- Will the recycling centers accept comingled material, or will material separation be required?
- Is there room on the site for separate dumpsters?
- Will any special handling of stored material be required (such as keeping drywall covered and dry)?
- Will this effort require double handling of material?
- Will each trade be responsible for clean up of their work?
- Who will control the clean up for the project?

- How do you account for material give back programs if the organizations accepting this material do not have the ability to weigh each piece of material received?
- Who will document this credit?
- Who is responsible for document upload to LEED Online?
- What will happen if someone fails to follow the recycling program?

MRc3: MATERIALS REUSE

Construction Submittal (Up to 2 Points)

The intent of this credit is to encourage teams to reuse materials and products. This effort reduces demand for virgin materials and reduces waste generated by the creation of those materials. This credit requires a team to use salvaged or refurbished materials for 5 percent (1 point) or 10 percent (2 points) of the total material costs for the project.

LEED defines material cost as the cost of all materials purchased for work found in the applicable specification sections. In addition, materials must be permanently installed elements. Nonfixed assets such as furniture can be included at the discretion of the team, but must be used consistently for all material related calculations (MR Credits 3–7). This credit excludes the cost of materials associated with mechanical, electrical, plumbing, fire protection, and vertical transportation equipment.

LEED defines reused materials as materials that come from a different project site or materials generated on-site that are used in a different way than originally installed. The reused material value can be based on the actual cost paid for the material or the material's replacement value.

Example

A project team would like to use salvaged brick as an exterior cladding element. The brick can come from three places: the project site (generated during demolition), a brickyard that specializes in used brick, or salvaged from another project site. Brick from the project site (generated during demolition) must be used in a different way than what it was used for originally. In other words, if the brick was part of a wall structure in the existing structure then in order for this material to count for this credit, it cannot be used for a wall element. Should you use this brick as paving material for paths in the landscape then it can be included for this credit. Since this material was not purchased as a part of the project, the cost must be calculated using fair replacement value.

If the team purchases reclaimed brick from a supplier, then there is no restriction on where it can be used in the project. The value of the material would be the purchase cost and can include all associated costs such as transportation, taxes, and markup.

If the brick is salvaged from a different project site, there are also no restrictions to its use.

Questions to Ask When Assembling the Estimate
- Where is this reused material sourced from?
- Is special handling required?
- Are there schedule implications regarding when the material will be available?
- Are there any latent issues with the material (e.g., lead paint)?
- Will the materials need to be cleaned or prepared before installation?
- Will the project architect require mock-ups or samples before this reused material is approved? If so, how much additional material will be needed to satisfy the approval process?
- Is there physical space on the project to store the salvaged materials if they need to be purchased before they are required on the project?

Case Study

This project was a restoration of an existing building from the late 1800s. Over time, the building fell into a state of disrepair and when the renovation began, most of the structural components (4" x 14" solid oak timbers) had to be removed and replaced. These timbers were approximately 25 feet long and were only decayed at one end (approximately 5 feet), leaving the remaining 20 feet sound. The team decided not to throw this material away and instead used these timbers to build the replacement stair from the basement to the first floor. They ripped the timbers down to size and used them for stair treads as well as the stair handrail.

The beams complied with this credit, because they were refabricated for a completely different use than originally intended. To determine the beams' value it was difficult to find a lumberyard that could price an oak timber 4" x 14" x 20' long. The team was able to use the cost of a like-size member but a different species (cedar) for LEED documentation purposes.

As mentioned earlier, materials contributing to this credit cannot also contribute to credits MRc1: Building Reuse, MRc2: Construction Waste Management, MRc4: Recycled Content, MRc6: Rapidly Renewable Materials, or MRc7: Certified Wood.

MRc4: RECYCLED CONTENT

Construction Submittal (Up to 2 Points)

The intent of this credit is to increase demand for building products that contain recycled materials. In order to achieve the credit, a contractor must purchase materials with recycled content such that the sum total of postconsumer plus half of the preconsumer content in all materials is at least 10 percent (1 point) or 20 percent (2 points) of the total materials' cost. While this language may be in the contract documents, contractors may dismiss these requirements, assuming that the designers have already selected materials that comply.

LEED defines recycled content in two ways: postconsumer and preconsumer. Postconsumer content moves through the retail or consumer stream and then is reclaimed to create a new product. Reinforcing bar made from junk cars is an example of postconsumer recycled content. Preconsumer recycled materials are created from waste generated by an industrial or manufacturing process. These materials are captured before they enter into the retail or consumer stream. Fly ash (a by-product of coal burning) used as a replacement for cement in concrete is an example of preconsumer recycled content. Recycled content is based on percentage, by weight, of the recycled materials contribution to the total product. For the fly ash, only the amount of fly ash is counted as recycled content, while the entire cost of the concrete must be included in the total project's material cost. The LEED definition also counts postconsumer and preconsumer recycled materials differently. Preconsumer materials are only counted at half of their value.

A contractor must create an action plan for this credit. Usually called out in the general conditions, the LEED action plan must contain:

- A list of the materials purchased that contain recycled content.
- The estimated total material cost for the project.
- The estimated value of each material that contains recycled content.

The value of recycled content is determined by the following equation:

$$\text{Value of total recycled content}(\$) = [\%\text{postconsumer} \times \text{material value}(\$)] \\ + \tfrac{1}{2}\,[\%\text{preconsumer} \times \text{material value}(\$)]$$

Example 1

Assume that a project is using a cubic yard of 4,000 PSI Concrete. This product is a typical "six-sack" mix and costs $100.00/yd. The breakdown of the weight of each element in a yard of concrete can be seen in the first table.

Rock =	25.00 lbs
Sand =	25.00 lbs
Water =	5.00 lbs
Cement =	40.00 lbs
Add mix =	5.00 lbs
Total Material Weight	100.00 lbs
Total Recycled Content	0 lbs

The structural engineer specifies 15 percent fly ash in the mix to contribute to MRc4: Recycled Content. This results in 15 percent of the cement being replaced with fly ash. The new breakdown of the weight for each element that goes into a yard of concrete can be seen in the second table.

Rock =	25.00 lbs
Sand =	25.00 lbs
Water =	5.00 lbs
Cement =	34.00 lbs
Fly ash =	6.00 lbs
Add mix =	5.00 lbs
Total Material Weight	100.00 lbs
Total Recycled Content	6.00 lbs of fly ash

Fly ash is considered a preconsumer recycled material. As a result, it only counts as half recycled content.

Total LEED Recycled Content = 3.00 lbs of ash

3.00 lbs fly ash/100 lbs per yard = 3% total recycled content

If 10 yards of concrete are used at $100/yard, the total material cost is $1,000. The recycled content of this material is 3 percent of $1,000, or $30.

LEED also allows for an alternate calculation methodology for supplementary cementitious materials (SCM). In this case, the total recycled content value may be considered as a percentage of the weight of cementitious materials only instead of the entire concrete mix design. In the previous example, the resulting calculation would be as follows:

3.00 lbs fly ash/(6.00 lbs fly ash + 34.00 lbs cement) = 7.5% total recycled content

Example 2

A project design calls for structural steel. The structural steel costs $1,000.00 per ton. A breakdown of the weight of each element in the steel (per ton) is below.

1,600.00 lbs	Postconsumer Recycled content (80%)
300.00 lbs	Preconsumer Recycled content (15%)
100.00 lbs	Virgin Steel (5%)

Using the formula for recycled content:

Value of total recycled content($) = [% postconsumer × material value($)
+ ½ [% preconsumer × material value($)]

Value = (80% × $1,000) + ½ (15% × $1,000) = $875.00

Questions to Ask When Assembling the Estimate

- Do the contract documents require the contractor to disclose costs of materials in the applicable specification sections?
- Have the recycled content requirements been included in each specification section that applies to this credit?
- Who is responsible for the documentation of this credit?

  Typically, the contractor must track material costs for the project for this credit. This can add time and possibly personnel to a project, so consideration must be given as to who will be responsible for this and how much time must be allocated to these activities.

- Do all subcontractors and suppliers understand the requirements of this credit?
- Will more expensive materials be needed to achieve this credit?

MRc5: REGIONAL MATERIALS

Construction Submittal (Up to 2 Points)

The intent of this credit is to increase demand for building materials and products that are extracted, processed, and manufactured locally, to encourage the use of indigenous resources and reduce environmental impacts related to transportation. The contractor must demonstrate that the materials used on a project are extracted, processed, and manufactured within a 500-mile radius from the project site. This credit requires a contractor to document the manufacture location, as well as extraction/harvest location. The credit thresholds are 10 percent (1 point) and 20 percent (2 points). If a material is not 100 percent regional, the percentage of regional contribution by weight is acceptable. Exemplary performance is awarded if a contractor achieves 40 percent and an additional point is achieved. However, it is documented in the Innovation in Design section of the rating system.

Questions to Ask When Assembling the Estimate

- Do the specifications give preference to regional materials?

    The specifications may be vague on this point, but the "front end" section of the specifications obligates the contractor to develop a plan as to how to achieve this and other material related credits. When assembling the estimate, a contractor must take care to identify those materials that have an effect on this credit.

- If regional materials are specified, will this result in a sole source proprietary material?

    In a hard-bid, product-based specification, multiple manufacturers are listed for any given product used in the job. On a non-LEED project, a contractor chooses the lowest-price product. On a LEED project, the contractor must also be concerned with achieving certain LEED points. This may narrow product choices included in the specifications.

- Is it less expensive to use vendors that are not local (according to the LEED requirements)?

    Even though a product is local, this may not mean that it will cost less. The estimator must assess all material choices to determine the best choice for price and LEED.

- Do you have a plan to buy at least 10 or 20 percent of all materials needed for the project from local sources?

- Do all of your subcontractors and suppliers understand the requirement of this credit?

- Do you have to make special considerations or price concessions to achieve this credit?

- Are local materials available in your area?

    If an estimator finds that the complete estimate does not contain enough material to fulfill this credit then the bid should include a clarification or explanation as to why the credit may not be achieved. Should a contractor wait to disclose this information, they may find themselves in a position to purchase materials not included in their original number to satisfy the performance requirements of this credit.

- Do the specifications allow for the use of local materials (is this the basis of the specification)?

Example

Assume that a project is using a cubic yard of 4,000 PSI concrete. This product is a typical "six-sack" mix and costs $100.00/yd. The breakdown of the weight of each element in a yard of concrete can be seen in the following table.

Rock =	25.00 lbs	Extracted at a local quarry (10 miles from the job site)
Sand =	25.00 lbs	Extracted from a local river (23 miles from the job site)
Water =	5.00 lbs	Municipal supply (11 miles from the job site)
Cement =	40.00 lbs	Extracted locally (107 miles from the job site)
Add mix =	5.00 lbs	From various locations (not local)
Total Weight =	100.00 lbs	

In addition, the concrete is manufactured at the local mix plant, 7 miles from the job site.

In this example, the entire mix is manufactured within 500 miles of the job site, but only a portion of the ingredients are extracted within that radius. As a result, only part of the concrete will count towards this credit. The rock, sand, water and cement make up the local materials and weigh a total of 95 pounds. As a result, the concrete is 95 percent regional which equates to $95/yard of regional content.

While the concrete did not add much to the recycled content credit (MRc4) it contributes a large amount to MRc5: Regional Materials.

Note

This example illustrates how the concrete contributes greatly to the regional credits. The structural steel used as an example in the recycled content section is often thought to contribute to this credit as well, especially when the mill is within 500 miles of the project site and the contractor has chosen a local supplier for the project. This is often not the case, however, as the origin of the scrap is unknown (steel can come from a variety of scrap sources: cars, washing machines, refrigerators, and so on). If the supplier is not doing any fabrication on the steel and is acting as a "pass-through" only, the point of manufacture is the mill. The point of extraction would not be able to be determined because the originating source of the steel scrap is unknown. As a result, this material cannot count toward this credit.

MRc6: RAPIDLY RENEWABLE MATERIALS

Construction Submittal (1 Point)

This credit encourages teams to use rapidly renewable materials, defined as products made from plants harvested within a 10-year cycle or less. Some examples of rapidly renewable materials are bamboo, wool, cotton, agrifiber, linoleum, strawboard, cork, and wheatboard. A team must incorporate these products so that the total contribution of rapidly renewable materials is at least 2.5 percent of the total materials cost for the project. Material contribution must be calculated by weight and only the percentage of rapidly renewable content counts toward achievement of this credit. Exemplary performance (and an additional point) is achieved if a contractor reaches 5 percent. However, it is documented in the Innovation in Design section of the rating system.

Contractors should be aware of potential warranty issues with these products. They may require unique installation methods or maintenance. Be sure to communicate this to the owner as well.

Questions to Ask When Assembling the Estimate
- Has a plan been developed to achieve this credit?
- Will any of this material entail long lead times?
- Do any of these materials require special handling?
- Are there warranty concerns?
- Do local subcontractors/suppliers have experience with these types of materials?
- Are all subcontractors and suppliers aware that they will be required to submit material cost breakdowns with their monthly pay requests?
- Who is responsible for the upload of information to LEED Online?

MRc7: CERTIFIED WOOD

Construction Submittal (1 Point)

The intent of this credit is to encourage environmentally responsible forest management practices. Teams are awarded this credit if they can demonstrate that a minimum of 50 percent of the wood used on their project comes from sources certified by the Forest Stewardship Council (FSC). The calculation of this credit differs from those of the other material related credits because it is calculated as a ratio of certified wood to the total wood used on the project. It is not compared to the total material costs as in the other material credits (MRc3–MRc6). Documentation must include a list of all new wood purchased for the project, identifying which items are FSC. The total FSC certified percentage is equal to the value of the FSC-certified wood divided by the value of all wood purchased for the project. In the case of an assembly product, such as a door, only the percentage that is FSC can be counted.

FSC's designation of "FSC Pure" or "FSC Mixed Credit" contributes 100 percent value to this credit. "FSC Mixed [NN%]" must be valued at the indicated percentage. In addition to a breakdown of FSC materials, the contractor must also submit Chain of Custody (CoC) certificates from all suppliers in the chain.

This credit applies to wood products that are permanently installed in the project (framing, dimensional framing, flooring, subflooring, wood doors, and finishes). However, if the contractor wishes to, they can include temporary wood (formwork, bracing, and the like), but then *all* such materials must be included in the calculation. Exemplary performance (and an extra point) is achieved if a contractor reaches 95 percent FSC wood. However, it is documented in the Innovation in Design section of the rating system.

Important Note on Chain of Custody

In order for a product to be classified as FSC for LEED purposes, there must be a Chain of Custody (CoC) from the forest to the point of installation. This means that each member of the supply chain must have CoC certification. Even if a party in the chain does not alter the product (such as a supplier or wholesaler), they must have a chain of custody.

Questions to Ask When Assembling the Estimate

- What is the plan for temporary wood?

    If a team intends to use temporary and permanent wood to achieve this credit, then care must be taken in purchasing the wood to ensure that chain of custody certificates can be provided by all the parties involved. The estimator should instruct all contractors and suppliers of wood about the requirements of this credit. Contractors and suppliers should also be informed about supplying financial information pertaining to the materials purchased.

- Do the specifications reflect the use of certified wood for all permanently installed wood?

    If a contractor is working on a project seeking this credit, they should identify every specification section that requires any type of wood material and determine if the requirements of certified wood have been included. FSC-certified wood can add cost to a project so it is critical that an estimator identify potential conflicts early in the process.

- Do the subcontractors/suppliers understand the requirements of FSC CoC requirements?

    In order to comply with this credit there must be a chain of custody certificate documenting each transaction from the forest to the final installation point. Many suppliers might commit to using FSC-certified wood products in the assembly of their goods, yet they will be unable to furnish chain of custody certificates because their facility has never been certified by FSC.

This credit is more than just using FSC wood; there must be a continuous CoC.

The following example will help to further explain the requirements of this credit. Here are the players used in this example:

- Allen owns a forest and has gone through the effort to certify his forest and forestry practices with the FSC. He has a Chain of Custody (CoC) certificate.

- Bruce owns a lumber mill and he works with Allen on a regular basis, so he too has had his manufacturing process certified by the FSC. He has a CoC certificate.

- Charles is a door manufacturer. Charles did not want to be left out of the green movement, so he had his manufacturing process certified by the FSC so he could sell FSC-certified wood doors on the market. He has a CoC certificate.

- Darwin owns a cabinet shop. He produces cabinets and ships them anywhere in the world. He will use any type or species of wood that is requested of him. He does not have a CoC certificate.

- Edward is a product representative and warehousing/distribution vendor that stocks and sells wood doors for a number of different door manufacturers. He represents the door company that Charles owns as well as other door manufacturers. He does not have a CoC certificate.

- Frank is a contractor who tendered on a project and was successful in his pursuit.

- George is the LEED consultant for the project. He is responsible for collecting the appropriate documentation needed for the LEED submission.

- Frank is asked to furnish documentation to support achievement of the MRc7, Certified Wood LEED credit. This credit requires that a minimum of 50 percent of all permanently installed wood products be constructed of FSC-certified wood.

Example 1

The wood products that were identified in the quantity survey are shown in the table.

Doors	$20,000.00
Cabinets	$8,000.00
Blocking	$500.00
Wall paneling	$4,000.00
Total	$32,500.00

In order to achieve the LEED credit, Frank needs to purchase a minimum of $16,250.00 of certified wood. Frank decides the easiest way to achieve the credit is to purchase FSC-certified wood doors for $20,000.00. Frank interviews Edward and asks if he represents a company that sells FSC certified wood doors. Edward responds that he can furnish FSC-certified wood doors produced by Charles's company. Frank places the order for the doors. During the construction phase, George asks Frank for the CoC certificates for the doors that had been purchased for the project. Frank in turn asks Edward for the CoC certificate.

Allen grows the timber and sells it to Bruce. At the time of that transaction, a CoC is exchanged along with the product as it is transferred from Allen (Allen is CoC certified) to Bruce. Bruce mills the timber into planks and sells the wood to Charles. At the time of that transaction, a CoC is exchanged along with the product as it is transferred from Bruce (Bruce is CoC certified) to Charles. Charles produces the doors and ships them Edward. At the time of that transaction a CoC is exchanged along with the product as it is transferred from Charles (Charles is CoC certified) to Edward. Frank purchases the doors from Edward and has them delivered to the project site. However, Edward does not have a CoC certificate. The chain of custody has been broken and for LEED purposes, the material used on site does not qualify toward the achievement of the LEED credit.

Example 2

The wood products that were identified in the quantity survey are shown in the table.

Doors	$20,000.00
Cabinets	$25,000.00
Blocking	$1,500.00
Wall paneling	$14,000.00
Total	$60,500.00

In order to achieve the credit, Frank needs to purchase a minimum of $30,250.00 of certified wood. Frank decides the easiest way to achieve the credit is to purchase FSC-certified wood cabinets and wall paneling. He contacts Darwin and asks if he can furnish FSC-certified wood for the custom cabinets and wood panels. Darwin states that he can use FSC-certified wood to make both the cabinets and the panels. However, even though Darwin is purchasing certified wood from Bruce and Bruce can furnish a copy of his CoC certificate, Darwin's shop is not certified by FSC so the chain of custody has been broken and the required documentation for the LEED submittal cannot be produced. Therefore, they will not be capable of achieving the credit.

Questions to Ask When Assembling the Estimate

- Are there schedule impacts if FSC wood is used?

    FSC materials are often special ordered. An estimator should determine the availability of FSC certified products to assess if there will be complications with the project schedule.

- Do the specifications reflect a preference to specific wood products or is it a performance-based specification?

    It is critical that the estimator review the manufacturers listed in a specification to determine if each of the products will conform to the requirements of this credit. Simply because a vendor or supplier is listed in a specification for wood products does not automatically mean that they will conform to the FSC requirements.

- Are all subcontractor and suppliers aware that they will be required to submit dollar breakdowns with their monthly pay requests?

- Who is responsible for the upload of information to LEED Online?

CHAPTER 10

Indoor Environmental Quality

Sustainable Sites, 23%

Water Efficiency, 9%

Energy and Atmosphere, 32%

Materials and Resources, 13%

Indoor Environmental Quality, 14%

Innovation and Design Process, 5%

Regional Priority, 4%

Humans spend almost 90 percent of their lives inside buildings. This category of points is focused on improving the quality of those indoor surroundings. Indoor Environmental Quality (IEQ) addresses the building's air quality, thermal comfort, daylighting, and views to the outdoors. In traditional buildings, many employees would welcome improvements to their working environment. Currently, facility managers spend a considerable amount of time addressing issues of occupant comfort.

In addition to the Materials and Resources category, this section of the LEED rating system heavily involves the contractor. When we discussed the LEED requirements as they may appear in the general conditions section of the specification, we called special attention to the requirement of the contractor's obligation to develop action plans addressing how they intend to achieve certain credits. Once submitted, reviewed, and accepted, these action plans become a part of the contract agreement and can be used to determine if the contractor has performed in accordance with the contract. As we detailed in that previous conversation, we cautioned the contractor that the creation of these action plans places certain performance related criteria onto what was intended to be a product specification. Contractors may find themselves accepting some level of design responsibility, depending on the level of detail contained in the action plan, how the specification was written, and the contractor's willingness to make product choices regarding product selection (what combination of materials will achieve thresholds prescribed in LEED). Contractors should be fully aware of the responsibility and the contractual obligation they are assuming when working on a LEED project. This is especially true when considering the prerequisites and credits of this category.

Description	Available	Submittal Phase
Prerequisite 1: Minimum Indoor Air Quality Performance	Required	Design
Prerequisite 2: Environmental Tobacco Smoke (ETS) Control	Required	Design
Credit 1: Outdoor Air Delivery Monitoring	1	Design
Credit 2: Increased Ventilation	1	Design
Credit 3.1: Construction Indoor Air Quality Management Plan—During Construction	1	Construction
Credit 3.2: Construction Indoor Air Quality Management Plan—Before Occupancy	1	Construction
Credit 4.1: Low-Emitting Materials—Adhesives and Sealants	1	Construction
Credit 4.2: Low-Emitting Materials—Paints and Coatings	1	Construction
Credit 4.3: Low-Emitting Materials—Flooring Systems	1	Construction
Credit 4.4: Low-Emitting Materials—Composite Wood and Agrifiber Products	1	Construction
Credit 5: Indoor Chemical and Pollutant Source Control	1	Design
Credit 6.1: Controllability of Systems—Lighting	1	Design
Credit 6.2: Controllability of Systems—Thermal Comfort	1	Design
Credit 7.1: Thermal Comfort—Design	1	Design
Credit 7.2: Thermal Comfort—Verification	1	Design
Credit 8.1: Daylight and Views—Daylight	1	Design
Credit 8.2: Daylight and Views—Views	1	Design
Section Total	**15**	

IEQp1: MINIMUM INDOOR AIR QUALITY PERFORMANCE

Design Submittal (Required)

The intent of this prerequisite is to establish a baseline for minimum Indoor Air Quality (IAQ) for all buildings seeking LEED certification. USGBC chose to use

ASHRAE Standard 62.1-2007, Ventilation for Acceptable Indoor Air Quality as this baseline unless the local code requirements are more stringent than the ASHRAE standard.

ASHRAE Standard 62.1 addresses all three methods of ventilation for a building: active, passive, and mixed-mode. Within the ASHRAE standard are compliance paths that a designer can use to demonstrate compliance under the guidelines of this prerequisite. This prerequisite requires a team to follow Sections 4 through 7 of the ASHRAE standard for a mechanically ventilated building, and systems must be designed using the Ventilation Rate Procedure. If a building is naturally ventilated, this prerequisite requires the design to comply with ASHRAE 62.1-2007, Paragraph 5.1.

This design submittal is straightforward. The design is either compliant with the LEED requirements or it is not. As long as the design is in compliance, the general contractor will have little to do with this credit. As with all other prerequisites and credits found in the LEED rating systems, a contractor should clearly state who is responsible for documenting each prerequisite and credit (calculations, LEED template and the upload to LEED Online) in the contract documents.

IEQp2: ENVIRONMENTAL TOBACCO SMOKE (ETS) CONTROL

Design Submittal (Required)

The intent of this prerequisite is to protect building occupants from secondhand smoke. LEED provides two compliance paths for commercial buildings and one compliance path for residential buildings.

For commercial buildings, the most straightforward compliance path is to follow Option 1, which requires a building owner to prohibit smoking in the building. If they allow outdoor smoking, then smoking areas must be at least 25 feet from doors, operable windows, and air intakes. Option 2 allows smoking within the building but only in designated areas. The designated smoking rooms must capture and evacuate Environmental Tobacco Smoke (ETS). In order to capture and evacuate ETS, the room ventilation must exhaust directly to the outside and be at least 25 feet away from any air intake. The room must be enclosed with impermeable deck-to-deck partitions and the system must negatively pressure the room with respect to adjacent spaces of the building. To demonstrate compliance, a 15-minute test must be conducted on each of the designated smoking rooms.

Owners of residential-type buildings must follow the residential case option. This option requires a building owner to prohibit smoking in all common areas of the building. As with the other two options, outdoor smoking must be at least 25 feet from doors, operable windows, and air intakes. Penetrations between units must be sealed. Doors leading from private areas of the building must be equipped with weather stripping, or the mechanical system must allow for negative pressure to adjacent spaces. To demonstrate compliance with all of these requirements, a 15-minute blower door test is required in each unit.

This prerequisite is a good example of how the owner and design team must collaborate to comply with LEED. While the design team is responsible for providing smoking areas, if applicable, it is the obligation of the building owner or operator to enforce the plan after construction is complete. If a building owner chooses to allow smoking inside their building, then the design and construction teams will expend additional effort and cost to comply with this prerequisite.

Questions to Ask When Assembling the Estimate

- At what phase of construction will the smoking ban go into effect?
- If the building owner intends to allow smoking in their building:
  - Does the design include deck to deck sealed partitions?
  - Does the design call for dedicated exhaust?
  - Is the exhaust discharge at least 25 feet away from an air intake?
  - Do you have the required testing included in the estimate?
  - Has the time for testing been incorporated into the project schedule?
  - On a residential building, are the doors leading to common hallways equipped with weather stripping?

Case Study

A recent ruling by USGBC shows how stringent certain LEED requirements can be. A team inquired (through a Credit Interpretation Ruling) whether smoking is allowed on a private balcony in a residential building. The ruling on the CIR was returned stating that it would be acceptable to allow smoking on the balconies as long as the smoking area is at least 25 feet away from a door, operable window, or fresh air intake. The lesson to be learned by this example is that the LEED requirements of this prerequisite are clear and are consistent. USGBC will not change the language of a credit or a prerequisite as a matter of convenience for an owner.

IEQc1: OUTDOOR AIR DELIVERY MONITORING

Design Submittal (1 Point)

The intent of this credit is to provide capacity for ventilation system monitoring by incorporating a permanent monitoring system. The system must provide feedback regarding the ventilation system performance. This feedback shows that the ventilation systems maintain the design minimum ventilation rates established as a baseline through EQp1. The system must be configured to generate an alarm or modulate the system automatically when operating conditions vary by more than 10 percent of the design parameters. LEED prescribes two separate compliance paths dependant on whether the building is mechanically ventilated or naturally ventilated. Systems in mechanically ventilated buildings must monitor carbon dioxide (CO_2) in all densely occupied spaces. LEED defines a densely occupied space as any room with more than 25 occupants per 1,000 square feet. The monitors in individual rooms must be placed in a position that is between 3 feet and 6 feet above the finished floor. In larger, nondensely occupied areas the monitor system can measure outdoor airflow rate. Naturally ventilated buildings must monitor CO_2. The monitoring devices are to be mounted between 3 feet and 6 feet above the finished floor and should alarm the facility staff when conditions are 10 percent above or below the design parameters.

Questions to Ask When Assembling the Estimate
- Are the CO_2 monitoring devices indicated on the drawings?
- Are the controls and the sequence of operation clearly detailed on the drawings?
- Will there be any special requirements for training of the facility staff?
- Will the CO_2 monitoring devices and controls have to be included in the commissioning process?

IEQc2: INCREASED VENTILATION

Design Submittal (1 Point)

The intent of this credit is to provide additional outdoor air ventilation. It is believed that increasing the amount of outdoor air inside a building is better for occupants in terms of comfort, well-being, and productivity. In the first prerequisite of this section, the baseline ventilation rates were established for the building using ASHRAE

62.1-2007. This credit requires the design to go above that standard by increasing the amount of outdoor air by at least 30 percent. Studies show a correlation between outdoor air rates and occupant comfort. Keep in mind, though, that an increase in outdoor air rates will, in most cases, adversely affect the energy performance of the building. In other words, a building that requires the mechanical system to condition a larger amount of outdoor air will consume more energy.

The credit provides a compliance path for both mechanically and naturally ventilated buildings. The design for a mechanically ventilated building calls for increasing the breathing zone ventilation rates by at least 30 percent above the baseline established in the prerequisite (ASHRAE 62.1-2007). The designers of natural ventilation systems must utilize the recommendations detailed in the Carbon Trust Good Practice Guide 237. The team must demonstrate that the design meets the Chartered Institution of Building Services Engineers (CIBSE) Applications Manual 10:2005, Natural Ventilation in Non-domestic Buildings.

Compliance with this design submittal is straightforward and a project's ventilation design will either be compliant with the LEED requirements or it will not. As long as the design is in compliance, the general contractor will have little to do with the documentation of this credit. As with all other prerequisites and credits found in the LEED rating systems, a contractor should clearly state what is in their scope of work.

IEQc3.1: CONSTRUCTION INDOOR AIR QUALITY MANAGEMENT PLAN—DURING CONSTRUCTION

Construction Submittal (1 Point)

The intent of this credit is to reduce indoor air quality problems created by construction and renovation activities. LEED encourages teams to incorporate these requirements in an effort to sustain the comfort and well-being of workers during the construction phase and the building occupants once the construction is complete. Achievement of this credit is directly dependent on the effort of the contractor. The contractor must develop and implement an Indoor Air Quality (IAQ) management plan during construction. The contractors working on the site must meet or exceed the requirements of the Sheet Metal and Air Conditioning Contractors' National Association (SMACNA) *IAQ Guidelines for Occupied Buildings Under Construction*, 2nd Edition 2007, ANSI/SMACNA 008-2008 (Chapter 3). The plan must also address protection of stored (on-site) or installed absorptive materials from moisture. Additionally, if the permanently installed air handlers are used during construction for climate control, minimum efficiency reporting value (MERV) 8 filters (or better) must be in place and they must be replaced immediately after construction but prior to occupancy.

The SMACNA IAQ guidelines consist of five control measures:

- HVAC Protection: Seal all ductwork when not in use to prevent dust from settling in the system. If the system is turned on during construction, ensure that MERV 8 filters or better are installed.
- Source Control: The team should specify and install low-emitting materials (covered in IEQc4.1 through IEQc4.4 of this book). In addition, areas where fuel-based equipment and tools are used should be well ventilated and fumes should be exhausted to the outside.
- Pathway Interruption: Protect pathways leading into the building or from construction areas to completed spaces. The contractor must prevent contamination of clean or occupied spaces from fumes and dust generated by construction activities. This may include isolating areas of material storage, placement of walk-off mats, or the use of temporary localized exhaust.
- Housekeeping: The contractor should clean and store porous materials out of water and minimize dust that may settle on stored materials.
- Scheduling: The master schedule for the project should reflect coordination activities, especially on projects with phased completion. The contractor must not disrupt occupied areas, must minimize IAQ impacts on those occupied areas, and must plan for a space or building flush-out.

FIGURE 10.1
HVAC Protection

FIGURE 10.2
Housekeeping (Absorptive Materials Covered and Palletized)

To document this credit, the team must submit a copy of the IAQ plan utilized during construction and preoccupancy. The LEED requirements called out in the general conditions section of the specification will obligate the contractor to develop this plan. Progress photographs must be taken during different phases of the construction indicating compliance. A list of the filtration media used during construction (if applicable) as well as confirmation that the filters were replaced immediately prior to occupancy must also be supplied.

Questions to Ask When Assembling the Estimate

- Who will be responsible for the creation of the IAQ plan?

    The plan may already be included in the specifications, but often the contractor will have to create it. If so, the contractor must understand the requirements for the plan. A contractor with little experience on LEED projects may see this credit as the responsibility of the mechanical trades/contractor purchasing and installing the equipment. In reality, protection of mechanical equipment is only one part of a CIAQ plan and the work of all trades will be affected. The plan must also address each of the other four SMACNA guidelines (source control, pathway interruption, housekeeping, and scheduling), which ultimately affect all aspects of a construction site.

- Which contractors will be responsible for compliance?

  The five areas addressed by the SMACNA guidelines include items that will affect the general contractor as well as all specialty contractors working on the site. During the estimating phase of the project, an execution plan for how and who will perform inspections should be determined. The mechanical contractor may be willing to inspect mechanical issues in the IAQ plan, but may not be comfortable reviewing other trades' work. This situation may duplicate inspection and reporting efforts. Early planning will save coordination time and questions during the construction phase.

- Do all contractors working on site understand the requirements pertaining to the use of low emitting materials?

  The individual credits pertaining to the use of low-emitting materials are found in other areas of the LEED rating system (IEQc4.1 through IEQc4.4). However, compliance with a low-emitting strategy will also have an effect on this credit.

- Who will be responsible for photo documentation?

- Who is responsible for completing the LEED template?

  If the general contractor chooses to divide the responsibility of compliance inspection between the general trades and the mechanical contractor, they must decide who is responsible for compiling this information and uploading it to LEED Online.

- Does the mechanical contractor understand that they will be required to keep all mechanical equipment covered or wrapped prior to and after installation?

  It is easy to obligate the contractor in the specification, but it is harder to enforce in the field. The site supervision should hold meetings with the labor supervisor for each trade throughout construction so that they understand the requirements and expectations for their work.

- Who will be responsible for housekeeping on the project?

- If the mechanical equipment is used during construction for climate control:
  - Will the specified equipment accommodate a MERV 8 filter?

    Not all equipment will accommodate these thicker filters. The estimator should review the design and ensure the equipment can handle this type of filter.
  - What maintenance has the contractor included for the filters?

    MERV 8 filters can be expensive. It is advisable to know how much maintenance is included in the mechanical contractor's estimate before award of the project.

○ Does the use of the mechanical equipment have any effect on the warranty?

○ Does the use of the mechanical equipment affect the commissioning activities?

If the equipment is to be used during the construction phase, the commissioning authority working on the project will want to witness prefunctional testing of the equipment before it is put into service.

• If a project is delivered through a phased completion:

○ How will pathway interruption be addressed?

○ Who will maintain protective measures between the phased areas?

IEQc3.2: CONSTRUCTION INDOOR AIR QUALITY MANAGEMENT PLAN—BEFORE OCCUPANCY

Construction Submittal (1 Point)

The intent of this credit, like IEQc3.1: Construction IAQ Management Plan—During Construction is to reduce indoor air quality problems from construction/or renovation activities. The previous credit was concerned with the IAQ during the process of construction. This credit continues the IAQ plan initiated during construction. It requires the development of an IAQ management plan for the preoccupancy phase of the project. LEED provides three separate compliance paths for teams seeking this credit. The first two deal with "building flush-out": the means of moving a certain quantity of outdoor air through the building. The remaining option is to test the quality of the air before occupancy.

The first option requires a flush-out before occupancy. LEED defines a complete flush-out as delivery of 14,000 cubic feet of outdoor air for every square foot of building space. The flush must be continuous and may not occur until all construction activities, including punch list, are complete. The building must be maintained at less than 60 percent humidity and at least 60 degrees Fahrenheit.

The second option allows the flush-out to be accomplished in two phases. This allows for a partial flush before initial occupancy with the remaining balance of the flush after occupancy. The requirement for humidity and temperature control is the same as well as the total amount of outdoor air (14,000 cubic feet) delivered. Under this scenario, the initial flush must provide 3,500 cubic feet of air per square foot of space prior to occupancy and the remaining balance (10,500 cubic feet) after occupancy.

The third option, air quality testing, is offered as an alternate to building flush-out. Teams may test the air quality of the building before the occupant takes over the space. As with the first two options, all construction activities must be complete before the testing can commence. Teams are instructed to use the Environmental Protection Agency's (EPA) method for determination of air pollutants. Air samples taken throughout the space cannot exceed contaminant thresholds for formaldehyde, particulates (PM-10), total volatile organic compounds (TVOC), 4-phenylcyclohexene (4-PCH), and carbon monoxide (CO). In addition to threshold limits for certain pollutants, the test must follow a certain methodology for both sampling and the aggregation of test results. The team may retest in the event of failure. LEED recommends flush-out before retesting.

In the first two compliance paths, a contractor will need to add time to the construction schedule. Additionally, the contractor must include the utility costs during the flush-out period if they are responsible for the payment of utilities during construction. If the construction schedule will not afford the time it takes to complete the flush-out, then money will have to be included in the budget for air testing.

When a contractor is planning a building flush-out, there are several components to consider including schedule, maintenance of mechanical systems, system capacity, and warranty. We will address each of these in detail.

Schedule: Often the bid documents will not address the systems' design related to outdoor air volumes. A contractor cannot calculate the flush-out time without knowledge of these features. Keep in mind that if the equipment cannot bring large amounts of outdoor air into the building, a flush-out could take weeks or longer. There simply may not be enough time in the project schedule to complete the flush. In addition, delays in the schedule could limit the amount of time available for the flush.

Maintenance of Mechanical Systems: The first compliance option requires delivery of 14,000 cubic feet of outdoor air per square foot of building area into the building before occupancy. The second compliance option requires delivery of 3,500 cubic feet of outdoor air before initial occupancy with the remaining 10,500 cubic feet of outdoor air after occupancy. Either approach to the building flush-out can take a considerable amount of time. During the process, the building occupant will not be in the building and someone must be responsible for changing filters and monitoring the system in general.

System Capacity: As mentioned previously, the amount of outside air the mechanical system can bring in, combined with atmospheric conditions, may not meet the temperature and humidity requirements of this credit.

Warranty: The time to deliver the volume of outdoor air required in this credit can be several weeks, if not longer. During this time, the mechanical system is running continuously and in most projects the system testing and balancing as well as commissioning has been completed. On a non-LEED project the completion of these activities would trigger the turnover and acceptance of the equipment by the owner and the start of the warranty period. On a LEED project, many owners do not wish to take acceptance of the equipment until the flush-out is complete. As a result, the contractor may be forced to purchase an extended warranty from the equipment manufacturer to replace the time the system was running but not accepted by the owner.

LOW-EMITTING MATERIALS

Four low-emitting credits in the LEED rating system pertain to materials used inside the building during construction. Each of these credits will be discussed in detail as they pertain to the preconstruction and estimating of a project. While each credit has its own compliance path, the intent is the same: "Reduce the quantity of indoor air contaminants that are odorous, irritating and/or harmful to the comfort and well-being of occupants and workers."

As we have discussed in Chapter 5, a project that is seeking LEED certification will likely contain some amount of LEED or sustainable requirements in the general section of the specifications. The section may be called "Section 018113—Sustainable Design Requirements." This specification section contains information that may be integrated into the rest of the contract documents, but often is not. Some specifications may even include a disclaimer that reads "Related Sections: Refer to the following sections for related work: Divisions 1 through 16 Sections for LEED requirements specific to the Work of each of those Sections. These requirements may or may not include reference to LEED." This disclaimer typically means that even if the specifications do not mention it, it is the responsibility of the contractor to know the requirements of LEED and execute the work accordingly. With low-emitting materials, specifications often include products that are no longer manufactured (i.e., adhesives, sealants, paints, and coatings) because they are carried over from a standard specification that has not been verified. Other times these products are not checked for compliance with the LEED performance standard. Regardless, the contractor is obligated to various responsibilities regarding the proper documentation and compliance to the LEED requirements.

As with many material related credits, the contractor must develop an action plan for these credits within a certain time from the notice of award. This action plan demonstrates how the contractor(s) will achieve the low-emitting credits. The action plan should address the submittal process associated with every low-emitting material used on the interior (inside the building envelope) of the project. In addition to the action plan, the contractor must also submit progress reports on a monthly basis. These progress reports must document compliance to the action plan.

It is the contractor's responsibility to base the low bid on the products contained in the specifications. On a non-LEED project the contractor selects the lowest cost product in the specification. As long as the contractor is not making unapproved substitutions, the work is within the contract agreements. On a project seeking LEED certification, the contractor must base the bid not only on low cost, but also on compliance with LEED performance criteria. The contractor must select the correct products, which may or may not be contained in the specification in the correct combination to comply with the LEED requirements as well as the lowest price.

When reviewing the specifications for a LEED project, a contractor must know if the products listed in the specifications abide by the requirements of each of these credits. These points illustrate the complication of mixing a product-based specification with the performance standards of the LEED rating system. In addition to knowing if specific materials in the specifications are compliant with the LEED credits, the estimator must also be aware of places where the contract documents do not call out specific materials but product submittals will be required for LEED compliance. For example, a drywall installer may have to submit product information for the gypsum wallboard, tape, and joint compound. However, the specifications will rarely address spray adhesives. Most installers carry spray adhesive with them on a job as a basic tool of the trade. On a non-LEED project this practice is acceptable. On a LEED project, this material requires a submittal, and must be reviewed for compliance with the LEED requirements before it can be used on the job.

IEQc4.1: LOW-EMITTING MATERIALS—ADHESIVES AND SEALANTS

Construction Submittal (1 Point)

For this credit, all adhesives and sealants used on the interior of the building (inside the weatherproofing) must comply with the following standards:

- All adhesives, sealants, and sealant primers shall comply with the South Coast Air Quality Management District (SCAQMD) Rule 1168. Volatile organic compound (VOC) limits correspond to an effective date of July 1, 2005.
- Any aerosol adhesives used on the project shall comply with Green Seal standard for Commercial Adhesives GS-36, dated October 19, 2000.

A contractor must provide a list of each adhesive, sealant, and sealant primer product used during construction inside the weatherproofing of the project. Typically, the contractor generates a spreadsheet that contains the manufacturer's name, the product name, the specific VOC data, and the corresponding allowable VOC for that particular product. The same information is required for all aerosol adhesive products used on the project.

Contractors need to use caution when pursuing this credit. The information required for this credit will include materials that, on a non-LEED project, do not require submittal and review. A contractor needs to look for adhesives, sealants, or aerosol adhesives being used regardless of whether the specification requires a submittal. The following are examples of how products can sneak onto a project site.

Example 1

An insulation installer is behind schedule. In an effort to make up lost time, the installer subcontracts installation of batt insulation to a contractor who will work the second shift so as not to disrupt any of the other construction activities. The insulation contractor never alerted the subcontractor to the LEED performance standards for the project. The installing subcontractor came to the site that evening and installed the insulation. The following morning, the general contractor's site management found an empty can of noncompliant adhesive. At this point, the contractor has to make a decision:

    a. The contractor can act like it never happened.

    b. The contractor can abandon the credit.

    c. The contractor can require the installing contractor to remove the material and replace it with a compliant adhesive.

The general contractor chooses the third option, and has the noncompliant material removed and replaced with the correct adhesive.

This example is offered to demonstrate the importance of descoping trade and subcontractors during the estimating phase of the project. All contractors selected to work on a LEED project must understand how their work can affect the LEED process. Estimators should take care to ask contractors if they have a detailed understanding of what will be expected from them during project execution.

Example 2

The contractor responsible for drywall installation has his first opportunity to work on a LEED project. He has read the contract documents and feels comfortable addressing everything called out in the specification. When his team mobilizes on site and starts installation of the wallboard, the tradesman uses a spray adhesive to temporarily affix a section of trim before it is permanently fastened. The tradesman is not aware that the product has to conform to the performance requirements of this credit. This material, something he considered a tool of his trade, required submittal and review before it could be used on a LEED project, even if it is not mentioned in the specification. Fortunately, a very small amount is used and the project site staff corrects the problem before it is used throughout the facility. As a result, the drywall contractor now supplies a compliant spray adhesive to the installers.

IEQc4.2: LOW-EMITTING MATERIALS—PAINTS AND COATINGS

Construction Submittal (1 Point)

For this credit, all paints and coatings used on the interior of the building (inside the weather proofing) shall comply with the following standards:

- Architectural paints and coatings must not exceed the volatile organic compound (VOC) limits established in Green Seal Standard GS-11, Paints, 1st Edition, May 20, 1993.
- Anti-corrosives and anti-rust paints must not exceed the VOC limit of 250 g/L in the Green Seal Standard GC-03, Anti-Corrosive Paints, 2nd Edition, January 7, 1997.
- Clear wood finishes, floor coatings, stains, primers, and shellacs must not exceed the VOC content limits established in SCAQMD Rule 1113, Architectural Coatings, January 1, 2004.

The documentation for this credit is similar to the previous credit, IEQc4.1: Low-Emitting Materials—Adhesives and Sealants. The contractor must produce documentation on each paint and coating used in the project. Typically, the contractor generates a spreadsheet that contains the manufacturer's name, the product name, the specific VOC data, and the corresponding allowable VOC for that particular product.

IEQc4.3: LOW-EMITTING MATERIALS—FLOORING SYSTEMS

Construction Submittal (1 Point)

There are two compliance paths a contractor can follow to achieve this credit. The first option requires all flooring material to be compliant with the following specifications:

- All carpet must meet the requirements of the Carpet and Rug Institute Green Label Plus Program.

- All carpet cushions must meet the requirements of the Carpet and Rug Institute Green Label Program.
- All carpet adhesives must meet the requirements of IEQc4.1: Low-Emitting Materials—Adhesives and Sealants, which includes a VOC limit of 50 g/L.
- All hard-surface flooring must be certified as FloorScore-compliant. Materials in this category are vinyl, linoleum, laminate, wood, ceramic, rubber, and wall base.
  - An alternative compliance path using FloorScore-compliant materials exists: 100 percent of noncarpeted finished flooring must be FloorScore certified and must constitute a minimum of 25 percent of the finished floor area
  - Mineral-based finished flooring materials (masonry, terrazzo, cut stone and the like) that do not incorporate organic-based coatings or sealants, and unfinished/untreated solid wood flooring can be considered compliant with this credit.
- Concrete, wood, bamboo, and cork floor finishes (sealer, stain, and finish) must meet SCAQMD Rule 1113, Architectural Coatings, January 1, 2004.
- Tile setting adhesives and grout must meet SCAQMD Rule 1168, effective July 1, 2005.

The second option requires all flooring elements installed in the interior of the building to meet the testing and product requirements of the California Department of Health Services Standard Practice for the Testing of Volatile Organic Emissions from Various Sources Using Small-Scale Environmental Chambers (including 2004 Addenda).

The contractor will be required to produce documentation on each flooring material used in the project. Typically, the contractor generates a spreadsheet that contains the manufacturer's name, the product name, the specific VOC data, and the corresponding allowable VOC for that particular product.

IEQc4.4: LOW-EMITTING MATERIALS—COMPOSITE WOOD AND AGRIFIBER PRODUCTS

Construction Submittal (1 point)

For this credit, all composite wood and engineered wood products used on the interior of the building shall contain no added urea-formaldehyde resins. Examples of composite wood and agrifiber include particleboard, medium-density fiberboard (MDF), plywood, wheat board, strawboard, panel substrates, and door cores. Laminating adhesives used to fabricate onsite and shop-applied composite wood and agrifiber assemblies must not contain added urea-formaldehyde resins.

Several types of formaldehyde are used in common construction materials, but formaldehyde occurs naturally in almost all wood-based products as well. A contractor must understand the difference in order to stay compliant with the requirements of this credit. Naturally occurring formaldehyde and phenol-formaldehydes are currently acceptable for LEED compliance. Manufacturer's product information must clearly state that the product contains no added urea formaldehyde in order to be acceptable. The terms "trace amounts," "negligible," or similar will not be accepted by a LEED reviewer.

A contractor is required to document the use of compliant materials on the job site. Typically, the contractor documents the materials used for all permanently installed composite wood or wood assemblies. This documentation includes manufacturer cut sheets and material safety data sheets for each product. When assembling the cost estimate for a project, the contractor should identify all areas where composite wood will be used. This credit does not fit neatly into the CSI division of wood. In addition to casework, doors, and millwork, this material may also be found in subfloors, wall backing (electrical/data/equipment rooms), nailers, and blocking.

IEQc5: INDOOR CHEMICAL AND POLLUTANT SOURCE CONTROL

Design Submittal (1 Point)

The intent of this credit is to minimize building occupants' exposure to potentially hazardous particulates and chemical pollutants. The requirements of this credit effect both elements of the building design and mechanical systems. First, each primary entrance is required have a permanent entry system to minimize pollutants from entering the building. These permanent systems can be grates, grilles, or slotted systems and must be a minimum of 10 feet in length. An alternate compliance path allows nonpermanent "roll-out" type mats, but the owner of the building must commit to a contract for weekly cleaning. Once all primary entrances to the building have been addressed, interior spaces where hazardous chemicals are stored must be constructed with deck-to-deck sealed partitions, must be negatively pressured with respect to adjacent spaces, and must have self-closing doors, and exhausted air may not be recirculated into the building. These locations might include garages, housekeeping supply closets, laundry rooms, science laboratories, art rooms, shops of any kind, and high-volume copying/printing centers. After the design team has accounted for these two components of the credit, the mechanical engineer must ensure that the air-handling equipment can accommodate a minimum efficiency reporting value

(MERV) 13 filter to treat outside and return air. The contractor must install these required MERV 13 filters immediately after construction and prior to occupancy.

LEED has defined this credit as a design submittal. However, a contractor may be involved with documentation. All design submittals must be reviewed at the end of the project to verify that nothing has changed during procurement and construction. The contractor must show that the MERV 13 filters were in place after construction and before occupancy. They may also be required to provide as-built drawings indicating that the storage rooms were constructed properly and exhaust ductwork is in place.

When assembling the estimate with this credit in mind, the contractor should make sure that all of the required criteria are contained in the design and contract documents. This may require a detailed conversation with the mechanical contractor and/or the equipment supplier to ensure that the air-handling equipment can accommodate a MERV 13 filter and that the installing contractor is aware that a new set of filters must be installed immediately prior to occupancy.

Questions to Ask When Assembling the Estimate

- Is a permanent walk-off system designed at each primary entrance? Are these systems 10 feet in length?
- Are all of the chemical storage areas designed with deck-to-deck partitions?
- Are there exhaust fans and ductwork for each of these storage rooms?
- Does the hardware schedule indicate door closers for these rooms?
- Has the air-handling equipment been specified with MERV 13 filters (supply and return)?
- Does the mechanical contractor have the required filter changes in their scope?
- Will the contractor be responsible for verifying this credit before final submission to USGBC/GBCI?

IEQc6.1: CONTROLLABILITY OF SYSTEMS—LIGHTING

Design Submittal (1 Point)

The intent of this credit is to provide lighting controls to the individual occupants of a building. Most people feel more comfortable in an environment where they can control the amount of light they need for various tasks. Individual lighting controls must be available to at least 90 percent of all building occupants. Shared or multi-occupant spaces must also be provided with lighting controls.

$$\text{Workstations/offices with lighting controls (\%)} = \frac{\text{Number of workstations/offices with lighting controls}}{\text{Total number of workstations/offices}}$$

Either a project's lighting design will be compliant with the LEED requirements of this design submittal or it will not. As long as the design is in compliance, the general contractor will have little to do with the documentation of this credit. As with all other prerequisites and credits found in the LEED rating system, a contractor should clearly state what is in the scope of work.

A lighting control is considered to be any type of device that a person can use to make adjustments to their lighting preference. This can be accomplished through wall switches, fixtures with dimming capability, or task lamps at a person's workstation. Rooms that are multi-occupant, such as conference rooms, or training areas must have the capability of control in the room in case the group wishes to make a lighting-level changes.

IEQc6.2: CONTROLLABILITY OF SYSTEMS—THERMAL COMFORT

Design Submittal (1 Point)

The intent of this credit is to provide building occupants with thermal comfort control. As with the lighting control credit (IEQc6.1), anecdotal evidence indicates that people who have control over their indoor environment are more comfortable, have a greater sense of well-being, and are more productive. This credit requires individual comfort controls for at least 50 percent of the building occupants. Controls must allow adjustments in at least one area of thermal comfort: temperature, radiant temperature, air speed, or humidity. USGBC defines a control as a thermostat, floor- or desk-level diffusers, or a radiant panel control. If a building has operable windows, the windows can be used as a control, but the controlled area is limited to 20 feet from a window and 10 feet to either side.

The design is either compliant with the requirements of this LEED credit or it is not. As long as the design is in compliance, the general contractor will have little to do with documentation for this credit. As with all other prerequisites and credits found in the LEED rating systems, a contractor should clearly state what is in the scope of work.

Example

While both of these credits are considered design submittals, some contractors may be burdened with work not in their scope due to a liberal interpretation of the performance-related LEED criteria in a product specification. A contractor may be asked to provide shop drawings for the mechanical equipment and systems in compliance with this credit. When the contractor included only equipment that was listed in the specification and the drawings, the submittal was returned as unacceptable. The contractor had read the general conditions and believed the statement "Additional LEED prerequisites and certain credits needed to obtain the indicated LEED certification depend on the Architect's design and other aspects of Project that are not part of the work of the Contract." The design review comments received indicated that the required amount of lighting controls was not sufficient per the LEED performance requirement, and for that reason the submittal was not complete. The contractor responded that he submitted equipment that was called for in the specification and that the nature of the design-bid-build award of the project did not require him to perform any type of design. The design representative responded back that the submittal would not be approved until it included information and devices that would support the design intent. The matter was brought to the owners.

After some deliberation and multiple meetings, the owners choose to forego the point. On one hand this was good news for the contractor, because he did not have to assume the responsibility and the cost to design the lighting system in compliance with the LEED requirements. Unfortunately, on the other hand the time that elapsed in reaching the conclusion forced the contractor to pay expediting fees in order to avoid schedule delays. In addition to this example, we have seen yet another case in which the LEED performance requirements were used to slow or refuse acceptance of a submittal for the lighting equipment and controls. The story is almost identical if mechanical equipment is exchanged for electrical equipment.

IEQc7.1: THERMAL COMFORT—DESIGN

Design Submittal (1 Point)

The intent of this credit is to design mechanical systems that allow for control of humidity levels within a building. USGBC cites that providing a comfortable thermal environment supports the productivity and well-being of building occupants. This credit requires the HVAC design and the building envelope to meet requirements of ASHRAE Standard 55-2004, Thermal Environmental Conditions for Human Occupancy. Teams must demonstrate compliance in accordance with section 6.1.1 of the ASHRAE standard, which can be used for passive, active, or mixed-mode ventilation systems.

This design submittal is one of the more straightforward LEED requirements. The design is either compliant with the LEED requirements for this credit or it is not. As long as the design is in compliance, the general contractor will have little to do with the documentation of this credit. As with all other prerequisites and credits found in the LEED rating systems, a contractor should clearly state what is in the scope of work.

IEQc7.2: THERMAL COMFORT—VERIFICATION

Design Submittal (1 Point)

The Intent of this credit is to incorporate appropriate controls into the mechanical system and provide for the ongoing verification of building occupants' thermal comfort. To achieve this credit, the design team must provide a permanent monitoring system to ensure that the building performance meets the comfort criteria as determined by IEQc7.1: Thermal Comfort-Design. In addition, the building owner/operator must implement a thermal comfort survey of occupants within 6 to 18 months after occupancy.

The LEED 2009 for New Construction rating system provides a list of items that must be included in the program:

1. The survey responses must be collected so that they are kept anonymous.
2. The survey must identify occupant's overall satisfaction regarding thermal comfort-related problems.
3. The measurements of the survey should be listed in such a way as to reflect relevant environmental variables in problem areas in accordance with the ASHRAE 55-2004 standard.

The survey must be followed up with corrective actions if the survey results indicate that more than 20 percent of occupants are dissatisfied with their thermal comfort.

This is another example of how the owner and design team must collaborate to accomplish compliance with a LEED credit. While the design team is responsible for providing a design in accordance with the applicable ASHRAE standard, it is the obligation of the building owner/operator to create a plan, write a survey, and be willing to correct problems should the survey indicate occupant dissatisfaction. This design submittal is straightforward. The design is either compliant with the LEED requirements or it is not. As long as the design is in compliance, the general contractor will have little to do with the documentation of this credit. Contractors must clearly state what is in their scope of work. Contractors working on LEED projects seeking this credit should not obligate themselves for the correction of issues arising from a survey response indicating that more than 20 percent of building occupants are dissatisfied with their thermal comfort.

IEQc8.1: DAYLIGHT AND VIEWS—DAYLIGHT

Design Submittal (1 Point)

The intent of this credit is to provide building occupants with a connection to the outdoors through introduction of daylight into regularly occupied spaces of the building. A compliant design must demonstrate that 75 percent of all regularly occupied spaces are daylit. The LEED 2009 for New Construction rating system states that in a commercial building, regularly occupied spaces are any interior location where a person sits or stands while working. The rating system provides a few options to demonstrate compliance with this credit.

> *Option 1:* Simulation. Perform a building simulation that demonstrates a lighting level of 25 foot-candles or more in at least 75 percent of regular occupied spaces. This option requires the computer model to perform the simulations using a maximum of 500 foot-candles under clear sky conditions on September 21 between the hours of 9 am and 3 pm.

> *Option 2:* Prescriptive. Side-lighting daylight zone: This area must achieve a calculated value where the visible light transmittance (VLT) and window-to-floor area ratio (WFR) of any daylight zone is between 0.150 and 0.180. There must also be sunlight redirection and/or glare-control devices for all windows in the space.

> Top-lighting daylight zone: This area is defined as the area directly beneath a skylight. The rating system limits this area to be no more than the outline of the skylight opening plus the area in each direction of the skylight, as defined by one of the following: 70 percent of the ceiling height, or half the distance to the nearest adjacent skylight, or the distance to any permanent hard wall partition. The design must achieve skylight roof coverage between 3 percent and 6 percent, and skylights must have a minimum VLT of 0.5. The distance between skylights can be no more than 1.4 times ceiling height of the space. If skylight diffuser is used then the measured haze value of the diffuser must be greater than 90 percent as tested by ASTM D1003 standard.

Option 3: Measurement. This option requires the team to demonstrate a minimum daylight illumination level of 25 foot-candles or higher in at least 75 percent of the space. The data measurements must be taken on a 10 foot grid.

Option 4: Combination. This option allows for the combination of compliance paths stated above. This compliance path allows a team to use any combination of the above calculation methods combined to document, at a minimum, 75 percent of the occupied space of a building.

As long as the design is in compliance, the general contractor will have little to nothing to do with the documentation of this credit. As with all other prerequisites and credits found in the LEED rating systems, contractors should clearly state what is in their scope of work.

FIGURE 10.3
Daylighting Strategies at William A. Kerr Foundation Office, St. Louis, Missouri

© Debbie Franke Photography, Inc.

IEQc8.2: DAYLIGHT AND VIEWS—VIEWS

Design Submittal (1 Point)

The intent of this credit is to provide building occupants with a connection to the outdoors by providing views to the outdoors from regularly occupied areas of the building. In order to achieve this credit the design team must document that there is a direct line of sight to the outdoors through the vision glazing. LEED defines vision glazing to be the portion of glass between 30 inches and 90 inches above the finished floor. A direct line of site must be demonstrated for 90 percent of occupants in all regularly occupied areas. One allowance is made for private offices. If 75 percent of the square footage of a private office has a direct line of sight, the entire space can be included in the calculation.

The design is either compliant with the LEED requirements or it is not. As long as the design is in compliance, the general contractor will have little to do in an effort to support the documentation of this credit. As with all other prerequisites and credits found in the LEED rating systems, contractors should clearly state what is in their scope of work.

CHAPTER 11

Innovation in Design

This category covers performance not addressed in other sections and rewards innovative strategies, exemplary performance, and team expertise in sustainable design. Five credit points are available in this category, including one for having a LEED Accredited Professional on the project team.

Description	Available	Submittal Phase
Credit 1: Innovation in Design	1–5	Design or Construction
Credit 2: LEED Accredited Professional	1	Design or Construction
Section Total	6	

IDc1: INNOVATION IN DESIGN

Design or Construction Submittal (1–5 Points)

The intent of this credit is to provide teams with the opportunity to be recognized for exceptional performance. This exceptional performance can be demonstrated in one

Sustainable Sites, 23%

Water Efficiency, 9%

Energy and Atmosphere, 32%

Materials and Resources, 13%

Indoor Environmental Quality, 14%

Innovation and Design Process, 5%

Regional Priority, 4%

of two ways. A team can go beyond the rating system's credits, or they can demonstrate exemplary performance in any of the existing credits within the rating system. Many of the points that are included in the rating system provide a threshold limit that a team must achieve in order to demonstrate exemplary performance.

Requirements

- Path 1: Innovation in Design (1–5 points)

    The team must submit in writing, and identify the intent of the proposed innovation credit, the proposed requirement for compliance, the proposed submittals to demonstrate compliance, and the design approach (strategies) that might be used to meet the requirements.

- Path 2: Exemplary Performance (1–3 points)

    An exemplary performance point may be earned for achieving the next incremental percentage or double the percentage threshold on an existing credit.

    ○ SSc2: Development Density and Community Connectivity

    Only applicable for teams pursuing Option 1. The project must demonstrate double the density within the calculated area *or* the average density within an area twice as large as that calculated for the base credit is at least 120,000 square feet per acre.

    ○ SSc4.1–4.4: Alternative Transportation

    Establish a comprehensive transportation management plan, which demonstrates a reduction in automobile use through any of multiple alternative options.

    ○ SSc5.1: Site Development-Protect or Restore Habitat

    Protect or restore 75 percent of the site area excluding the building footprint or 30 percent of the total site (including footprint).

    ○ SSc5.2: Site Development—Maximize Open Space

    Option 1: Provide 50 percent more open space than zoning requirements.
    Option 2: Provide open space equal to two times the building footprint.
    Option 3: Provide 40 percent of the site area as open space.

    ○ SSc6.1: Stormwater Design—Quantity Control

    Document a comprehensive approach to capture and treat stormwater runoff demonstrating performance beyond the credit requirements.

    ○ SSc6.2: Stormwater Design—Quality Control

    Document a comprehensive approach to capture and treat stormwater runoff demonstrating performance beyond the credit requirements.

    ○ SSc7.1: Heat Island Effect—Nonroof

    Option 1 and/or Option 2 must be met at 100 percent.

o SSc7.2: Heat Island Effect—Roof

  100 percent of roof area must be covered by a green roof system (excluding equipment, solar panels or skylights).

o WEc2: Innovative Wastewater Technologies

  Achieve a 100 percent reduction in potable water use for sewage conveyance or 100 percent on-site treatment.

o WEc3: Water Use Reduction

  Projects must demonstrate a 45 percent reduction in projected potable water use.

o EAc1: Optimize Energy Performance

  Applies only to buildings using Option 1, Energy Modeling. New buildings must achieve 50 percent and existing buildings must achieve a 46 percent energy use reduction.

o EAc2: On-site Renewable Energy

  15 percent or more of annual building energy cost must be provided by on-site renewable sources.

o EAc6: Green Power

  Purchase 100 percent of needed electricity from renewable sources.

o MRc2: Construction Waste Management

  Divert 95 percent or more of construction waste from landfill.

o MRc3: Materials Reuse

  Utilize reused materials for 15 percent or more of the total material cost of the project.

o MRc4: Recycled Content

  Incorporate recycled content materials for 30 percent or more of the total material cost of the project.

o MRc5: Regional Materials

  Incorporate regionally harvested, extracted, and manufactured materials for 30 percent or more of the total material cost of the project.

o MRc6: Rapidly Renewable Materials

  Utilize rapidly renewable materials for at least 5 percent of the total materials value of the project.

o MRc7: Certified Wood

  Incorporate FSC certified wood for 95 percent or more of the total wood products value for the project.

o IEQc8.1: Daylight and Views—Daylight

  Provide daylighting strategies for 95 percent or more of all regularly occupied areas.

○ IEQc8.2: Daylight and Views—Views

Meet two of the following four measures:

◻ 90 percent or more regularly occupied spaces have multiple lines of sight to vision glazing in different directions, 90 degrees apart.

◻ 90 percent or more regularly occupied spaces have views to at least two of the following three: vegetation, human activity, objects at least 70 feet from exterior glazing.

◻ 90 percent or more regularly occupied spaces have access to unobstructed views within distance of three times the head height of vision glazing.

◻ 90 percent or more regularly occupied spaces have access to views with a view factor of three or greater.

Projects may only achieve a total of 3 points through the exemplary performance compliance path.

IDc2: LEED ACCREDITED PROFESSIONAL

Construction Submittal (1 Point)

This credit supports and encourages the design integration required by a LEED green building project by ensuring that a LEED professional is included as a primary member of the team. The LEED Accredited Professional also serves to streamline the application and certification process.

This credit has been designated as a construction submittal. The LEED AP may be any principal participant of the project team, but the credit remains the contractor's responsibility to document. The following information is required for submission to USGBC/GBCI:

- Name of LEED AP
- Name of LEED AP's company
- Brief description of his or her role on the project team
- Copy of LEED AP certificate

CHAPTER 12

Regional Priority

The Regional Priority section is an entirely new credit category in LEED 2009. The intent of this category is to give preference to regional or geographic environmental priorities. Like the Innovation and Design category, these points are in addition to the 100 "base" points found in the rating system. USGBC enlisted the assistance of all regional chapters to choose the credits for regional priority. Instead of creating four new points for each region, the working groups weighted existing LEED credits as those that were most important for their particular region.

Description	Available	Submittal Phase
Credit 1: Regional Priority	1–4	Design or Construction
Section Total	4	

Sustainable Sites, 23%

Water Efficiency, 9%

Energy and Atmosphere, 32%

Materials and Resources, 13%

Indoor Environmental Quality, 14%

Innovation and Design Process, 5%

Regional Priority, 4%

RPc1: REGIONAL PRIORITY

Design or Construction (1–4 Points)

The requirements for this credit are based on the zip code of the project location. To document compliance with any one of the four regional priority credits, a team must first demonstrate compliance and achievement with the listed credit within the rating system. If a project achieves these particular credits, they will automatically qualify for an "extra credit" under Regional Priority. For any given zip code, a total of six credits have been designated as Regional Priority, but a team can only be awarded four of the six. It is also important to note that under the current version of the LEED 2009 rating system, the Regional Priority credits are not available to projects outside of the United States.

Example

Navy League Building
Arlington, VA 22201

- SSc5.1: Site Development—Protect or Restore Habitat
- WEc2: Innovative Wastewater Technology
- WEc3: Water Use Reduction
  40 percent
- EAc1: Optimize Energy Performance
  40 percent (New Building)/36 percent (Existing Building)
- EAc2: On-site Renewable Energy
  1 percent
- MRc1: Building Reuse
  75 percent

Alberici Headquarters
St. Louis, MO 63114

- SSc1: Site Selection
- SSc5.1: Site Development—Protect or Restore Habitat
- SSc6.2: Stormwater Design—Quality

- EAc2: On-site Renewable Energy
  7 percent
- MRc2: Construction Waste Management
  75 percent
- MRc5: Regional Materials
  20 percent

PART III

Case Studies

CHAPTER 13

Case Studies

PROJECT 1: William A. Kerr Foundation Office

Project type: Commercial building
Project size: 5,000 square feet
Project delivery: Integrated delivery
Project owner: Private
LEED certification: LEED-NCv2.1 Platinum

Introduction

This circa 1895 building was originally built as a bathhouse because of its location atop a natural mineral spring. Through the many years of the building's life, it functioned first as a bathhouse, then a warehouse and an automobile paint shop. Prior to the purchase by its current owner, the building was in desperate need of repair.

The owners saw something in this building that no developer had yet to see: an opportunity. They learned that through the renovation of this building, they could communicate their mission, support the community, and have fun all at the same time. None of the owners had any real practical experience with commercial building renovation, which proposed one of the first challenges of the project. They had to assemble a team of professionals to assist them in making their dream a reality. The owner hired a local architectural firm to work with the sustainability consultant, to begin the initial conceptual design work for the building. Soon after the conceptual design was underway, the owner made the decision to hire a local design-build contractor to work with the team at this early stage. The construction firm was chosen to supply the construction expertise the team would need to complete this renovation and restoration. The owner made a commitment to sustainable design and construction, and to demonstrate this commitment, began the process of seeking to LEED certify this project. The team that was assembled to deliver this project saw as many possibilities in the building as the trustees had seen when the decision was made to purchase the building. It was the start of a truly integrated delivery team; the owner, designer, contractor and sustainability consultant all worked together from the onset to give new life to this building.

One of the goals of the owner was to create office space and offer the building and interior spaces as a learning center for those seeking to understand how to incorporate sustainability into their buildings. The building is located near a bicycle trail system. The location, combined with the owner's interest in bicycling, provided a platform to support both a passion for bicycling and an avenue for learning. Once in operation, the building would provide:

- A staging area for bicycle rides
- Office space
- A local learning center for sustainable buildings
- A gathering place for all nonprofit and charitable organizations

This location, ideal due to its proximity to the trails, also provided additional opportunities for the owner to reinvest in building stock that is often neglected by developers.

The goal to have the building become LEED certified quickly sharpened the team's focus. Every member of the project team believed in the building and had a strong desire to find the full potential of this small but greatly interesting building. Instead of struggling for ways to capture or keep a point, the team found innovative ways to employ strategies that added points to the scorecard at little or no additional cost to construction. Through the combined design and construction knowledge of the team, and led by the vision of the owner, the team found themselves seeking and eventually achieving a Platinum level certification for the building.

The initial phase of the renovation was completed in December 2006, and became the first LEED Platinum building in the City of St. Louis.

The team faced several major challenges in the process of the renovation:

- The building is located in a blighted area of the city, which created a security challenge for the construction team.
- The extent of weather damage and damage due to neglect could not be determined at the time of initial assessment on the property.
- The team had to deal with remediation of both perceived and real environmental contaminants in the process of construction.
- The structure that at one time abutted this building had been demolished long ago, exposing the entirety of the north side of the building to conditions it was never intended to endure.
- The building had been constructed in two phases utilizing two completely different building methodologies.

Scope

The approximately 5,000-square-foot LEED Platinum project incorporates the following features:

- Office space
- Meeting and educational space
- Storage space
- Unfinished "future" space
- Small catering/event kitchen
- Garden roof terrace

Additional goals of the project included:

- Use of renewable energy sources
- Restoration of the beauty of this historic building

Project

Sustainable Sites

The team faced extreme difficulties working with this site. The original building was constructed as a "zero lot line" building; it had no open space adjacent to the structure.

During the process of construction, the owner purchased a 20-foot easement along the north side of the building. This purchase allowed the team to incorporate pervious paving for low-emitting/fuel-efficient and carpool vehicles and a rain garden to slow and treat the stormwater runoff. These efforts, combined with the owner's desire to demonstrate other sustainable techniques, including a green roof, allowed the team to explore many strategies that were not available when the project first started.

Water Efficiency

Water efficiency in a small office space is difficult to achieve, and highly efficient fixtures can be difficult to source. The project team maximized the amount of water efficiency by incorporating these strategies:

- Dual-flush water closets
- Low-flow lavatories in the restrooms
- Low-flow showerhead in the changing facility
- No potable water use for irrigation

While not able to achieve a 50 percent reduction in potable water used for sewage conveyance (WEc2), the team achieved all remaining credits in this category.

Energy and Atmosphere

Demonstration and learning were cornerstones in the project design. The team worked to design a highly efficient system while remaining within a conventional system budget. The goal was to allow people to come and learn about these systems in an effort to replicate them in their own projects. The team chose to use whole-building simulation for energy modeling. An energy model was used to help provide information about the energy efficiency of the building systems, and was also used for evaluation of construction options during the value-engineering phase of the construction. The owner demonstrated a strong desire to incorporate renewable energy sources into the building systems. Active solar and wind-generated power contributes close to 20 percent of the building's energy needs. The commissioning process utilized by the team in association with the monitoring process provides yet another opportunity for others to learn from this project.

Materials and Resources

Recycling, reuse, and locally sourced materials were a part of the project's everyday life. The first of these efforts was demonstrated by the owner's selection of an existing building. All of the existing building shell was left in place. Over 80 percent of the construction waste was diverted from the landfill by way of recycling centers. Cardboard, paper, glass, plastic, and metals were recycled. Waste wood was reused on-site wherever possible and workers were allowed to take scraps for home projects. Some of the existing elements of the building, such as framing timbers, were found to be partially unsound due to neglect and decay. The team reworked the remaining sound portion of these timbers, refurbishing them into stair treads and risers. The owner supported the local Habitat for Humanity's ReStore through the purchase of cabinets and other items used to finish the space. The countertops in the catering kitchen were made from material reclaimed from a local stone mason's scrap pile. The access floor was reclaimed from a local source. Recycled materials were used in many of the building's materials including insulation, synthetic gypsum, and carpet. Over 50 percent of the construction materials were sourced locally.

Indoor Environmental Quality

The various uses of the building over its past life allowed the project team a fresh start. Operable windows were added to the building along the north elevation to allow fresh air and views to the outdoors for all of those in the space. Stationary and operable skylights were incorporated into the roof design, allowing an abundance of natural daylight and natural ventilation. The team utilized an underfloor air distribution system to provide ventilation and allow for a more efficient system in this sustainable building. All of the contractors working on site followed a stringent no/low-emitting VOC policy and CIAQ program during construction. The team is confident the indoor air quality provided for clients and staff is the freshest and healthiest possible.

Innovation in Design

Education and Outreach: During the construction phase of the project, the team allowed local groups interested in green buildings to visit and tour the site. Since construction completion, the owners of the building invite all interested groups to come and learn about sustainability, bicycling, and the work of the owner. Educational signage has been incorporated throughout the space, which explains to visitors how unique this project is and how the team incorporated ideas of sustainability into every facet of the project.

Green Cleaning Program: The owner made a commitment to use a Green Cleaning Plan in the new space as well as biodegradable, recycled paper products.

Exemplary Performance Recycled and Regional Materials: Other innovation credits were achieved through the project's exemplary performance in the Materials and Resources credits, MRc4: Recycled Content and MRc5: Regional Materials.

Lessons Learned

Timing: This project followed a unique timeline in that the building owner purchased the building prior to performing a substantial investigation of the soundness of the physical building, developing a move-forward plan for the required renovations or establishing goals for the project (schedule, budget, team members). An architect was first hired who had a passion for the project but little experience with delivering a project of this type through an integrated design or delivery methodology. Several months after the owner had been in discussions with the architect they brought on a sustainability consultant to assist with the overall strategy of the project. By the time the consultant was brought on board, a contract had been issued for the integrated photovoltaic panels and elements of the vegetative roofing system. The project was a success. However, it is best if a project starts out with established goals.

Cost: The owner had not established a budget for the project at the start of the process. Little information regarding the structural condition of the building was available and the owner really had not made a firm decision for the end use of the building. This made it difficult to benchmark whether the team completed the project on budget. At the end of the project the owner did comment that he felt that he had spent more money then he had originally anticipated but he loved the building and did not regret the money that had been spent. Because the owner did not have a complete structural review of the building performed before or soon after the purchase, the team encountered several unforeseen conditions that added both scope and cost to the project. The roof structure had to be repaired and reinforced for the photovoltaic panels and the green roof system. The joists supporting the first floor had to be replaced due to several years of neglect. In order to make the building weather tight, the north exterior wall of the building had to be reconditioned both above and below grade. As an early adopter of LEED, the owner sometimes felt costs were overly high because there were so few vendors of the new green technologies from which to choose.

Team: The assembly of the final delivery team happened somewhat piecemeal. The one thing that all members of the team had in common was a passion for the project. They worked together always looking for opportunities to bring innovative ideas to the project. This sprit enabled the team to start the project with a LEED goal of Silver and complete the project with the achievement of Platinum.

PROJECT 2

Project type: Commercial/Healthcare
Project delivery: Design-build/design-bid-build
Project size: Two buildings, less than 4,000 square feet each
Project owner: Private
LEED certification: LEED-NCv2.2 Certified

Introduction

The owner of these two buildings made an organizational commitment to sustainable design and construction and sought to LEED certify all of their new facilities. Both of the projects were completed in October 2006 and at the time were anticipated to be among the first LEED certified health clinics in the local area. The two buildings followed the same basic design with the biggest difference being their physical location. The owner used the same delivery team on both projects as a way to deliver these facilities in the most efficient manner.

The goal of the team was to reduce and, to the greatest extent possible, eliminate the impact of these buildings on the natural environment. The design element of a glass curtain wall in the lobby allows for an abundance of natural light. The incorporation of natural plants and soft music create a soothing atmosphere for visitors and patients waiting in the lobby. These and other elements created a healthful and comfortable environment for visitors.

The team believed that there was a direct correlation between the mission of the owner and the philosophy of sustainable design and construction practices with their building projects. The buildings would incorporate environmentally friendly, sustainable materials, with mechanical systems and lighting creating a truly sustainable building block for the community.

The team faced several major challenges early in the process of construction:

The location of the buildings was less than ideal. The sites were located in an area that was below the 100-year-flood elevation. Unfortunately, this was not discovered until the design-build contractor was engaged to advise the client on issues of sustainability. While this caused considerable discussion about the site, the environmental repercussions and the cost implications to the project, the owner had already made a substantial financial commitment and it was decided that the project should move forward.

An important feature of both sites was their proximity to the community. This adjacency enables pedestrian travel, minimizes driving for clients, and takes advantage of existing public infrastructure.

Both locations were very small sites. While this was desirable in most respects, it presented a challenge in achieving stormwater management and site development credits.

If the team was to capitalize on the available energy related credits, the buildings required a dramatic reduction of lighting power densities as compared to a traditional health clinic.

Scope

Each of the approximately 3,500 square-foot buildings included a reception area, children's play area, exam rooms, office spaces, a nurse's station, laboratory and X-ray spaces, a conference room, and a staff lounge.

Project

Sustainable Sites

Working with these particular sites posed some problems for the project team. These sites were less than 5 feet above the 100-year flood plane. While the sites were brought up to the appropriate elevation for the governing authority, they did not meet the requirements for SSc1: Site Selection. The project team took advantage of reducing the impacts of automobile use by providing adequate parking and designated spaces for fuel-efficient vehicles. These reserved parking spaces are near the main entrance and give the conscientious driver prime parking. Local zoning requirements would not allow for a change to the mandated parking counts for the site. Therefore, the team was unable to achieve SSc4.4: Alternative Transportation—Parking Capacity. However, the owner made the decision to further exemplify the mission for an assured better tomorrow by encouraging carpooling anyway.

Water Efficiency

A high level of water efficiency can be difficult to achieve in healthcare facilities. This project maximized the amount of water efficiency by incorporating three strategies:

1. Pressure-assisted flush water closets
2. Low-flow lavatories in the restrooms
3. The use of a water-free hand-sanitizing system

Because the staff is required to wash their hands after each process, the amount of water saved by not using the exam room faucets has a dramatic impact on the amount of overall water usage, which translates into an actual financial savings to the owner.

Energy and Atmosphere

The team chose to use whole-building simulation for energy modeling. This information was used for considering construction options during the value-engineering phase of the construction. This system supports the commissioning process and adds validity to the measurement and verification process.

Material and Resources

Recycling and reuse is a part of the owner's mission. Over 50 percent of the construction waste was diverted from the landfill by way of recycling centers. Cardboard, paper, and metal were recycled. Waste wood was reused on site wherever possible and workers were allowed to take scrap wood for home projects. Recycled materials were used in the building materials' make-up. Structural steel, concrete, and aluminum framing all include large percentages of recycled content. Additionally, over 30 percent of the construction materials were extracted, processed, and manufactured regionally.

Indoor Environmental Quality

The owner knew that it made sense to operate in a sustainable building. In addition to energy cost savings over the life of the building, sustainable facilities offer occupants healthy indoor environments, benefiting both visitors and staff. A construction indoor air quality management plan was utilized during the construction phase and low-emitting adhesives, sealants, paints, coatings, and carpet systems were used exclusively.

Innovation in Design

The goal of becoming one of the first LEED certified facilities in the local area guided the team to a number of innovations on this project.

Green Cleaning Program: The owner made a commitment to use green cleaning products and practices in all of their clinics.

Exemplary Performance, WEc3: Water Use Reduction: Another innovation credit was earned from the exceptional performance in water use reduction.

Lessons Learned

Team: The owner made a prudent decision when hiring the same team for both of these projects. Members of the team did not have to go through the learning curve associated with most projects because as a team they had delivered several projects in the past. This familiarity allowed for the needs of the discipline engineers to support the aesthetic desires of the architect and the owner.

Cost: The owner of these two buildings was no stranger when it came to the topic of cost or time required to deliver this type of project. In the past they had built other facilities that were very similar to these buildings and had a high expectation that the team would complete the projects on time and within budget. While the owner had experience with constructing facilities such as these, these were their first LEED buildings. The delivery team completed both of these buildings on time, to the LEED certification level desired by the owner and at the owner's traditional construction budget.

LEED: These two buildings were designed by the same team, followed the same floor plan, were built by the same contractor, were constructed with the same materials, were energy modeled by the same person, were guided by the same sustainability consultant, and sought the same LEED credits. The biggest difference between the two buildings was the site location. It would stand to reason that when the projects were submitted for review by USGBC that the comments or objections returned by the reviewers for these two projects would be the same. In actuality the team received different comments and objections on both projects. The review comments were not radically different from one another but there were still differences in the way the reviewer analyzed the documentation. It is important to remember that human beings are performing the documentation review. Equally important is to remember that there are several people who are contracted by USGBC to perform these reviews and while they attempt to be impartial and objective in their reviews, each person can interpret the provided information differently. At the end of the process both buildings received the same level of certification. However, this proves that no two projects are ever the same!

PROJECT 3

Project type: Commercial/Retail

Project size: 30,000 square feet

Project delivery: Design-bid-build

Project owner: Private

LEED certification: LEED-NCv2.2 Gold

Introduction

The owner jumped at the opportunity to design and build this 30,000-square-foot facility using "green" architecture with the intent of certifying the building as a LEED project. The owner's family looked forward to demonstrating their environmentally conscious commitment with the same integrity that has always been the foundation of their business.

One of the goals of the project team was to create a one-of-a-kind facility, hopefully becoming one of the first LEED certified buildings of its type.

The building accommodates:

- A full-service retail area
- Maintenance shop
- Apparel shop
- Administration offices
- A local learning center for sustainable buildings
- A gathering place for enthusiasts

The goal to have the building become certified by USGBC quickly transformed the team. Every member of the project team believed in the building and had a strong desire to realize its full potential.

The construction phase of the project was completed in December 2007, and became one of the first LEED certified buildings in the local area.

Scope

The 33,000-square-foot building LEED Gold building includes the following:

- State-of-the-art maintenance shop
- Retail space displaying stock, parts, and accessories
- Design center
- Apparel shop
- Stacked inventory storage
- Administrative offices on the second level
- Customer lounge

Project

Sustainable Sites

The building is sited within the naturally landscaped grounds, which contains native grasses, plants, and drought-tolerant shrubs and trees. The natural look, in lieu of a manicured lawn, limits maintenance and water use and promotes points for LEED.

Water Efficiency

Water efficiency in the building was difficult to achieve. The project is located in an area where the use of water-free fixtures is not compliant with local building codes. The project team maximized the amount of water efficiency by incorporating these strategies:

- Dual-flush water closets
- Low-flow lavatories in the restrooms
- Low-flow showerhead in the changing facility
- No potable water used for irrigation

The team achieved all credits in the Water Efficiency category with the exception of WEc2: Innovative Wastewater Technologies.

Energy and Atmosphere

The team worked to design a highly efficient system, while retaining a conventional system budget. People can come and learn about these systems in an effort to replicate them in their own projects. The team chose to use whole building simulation for energy modeling. The entire building is constructed using an energy-efficient structural wall system, Insulated Concrete Forms (ICF), providing an insulation R-value of 40. Overall, the building is over 24 percent more energy efficient than baseline.

Materials and Resources

The interior of the building moves beyond the standard hard-edge industrial appearance of many buildings of this type to a sophisticated, refined design using a palette of muted color, natural slate and bamboo wood flooring, specialty coatings in the display areas, and a combination of lighting means. Natural light through the northwest showroom windows and over 40 solatubes are supplemented by the computer-controlled lighting system, which provides an energy savings mode for all of the artificial light fixtures.

Over 50 percent of the construction waste was diverted from the landfill by way of recycling centers. Structural steel, synthetic gypsum, carpet, and other materials were selected to incorporate recycled content. Over 44 percent of the construction materials were sourced locally.

Indoor Environmental Quality

Stringent VOC limits were placed on products such as adhesives and sealants used throughout the building. The well-insulated envelope coupled with an advanced mechanical system allowed a reduction in the size of the equipment. The technicians in the maintenance shop work on a concrete slab heated with a hydronic radiant water system. This system burns used motor oil as fuel. All of the contractors working on site followed a strict CIAQ program during construction.

Innovation in Design

Education and Outreach: Educational signage has been incorporated throughout the space explaining to visitors how unique this project is and how the team incorporated ideas of sustainability into every facet of the project. The owner provides building tours to all interested groups.

Green Cleaning Program: The owner's management team made a commitment to use only green cleaning products in their new space as well as biodegradable recycled paper products.

Exemplary Performance: Other Innovation in Design credits were earned from the exemplary performance in MRc4: Recycled Content and MRc5: Regional Materials.

Lessons Learned

Timing: This project followed a typical timeline. An architect was hired for the project before a decision was made to seek LEED certification. The project was in the midpoint of the design phase when a contractor was selected to assist in the preconstruction phase of the project. The contractor recognized that there was an opportunity to add value through their services and began a discussion of sustainability and possible LEED certification. A sustainability consultant was added to the team at this stage to assist with the overall strategy for the project. It is always best if a project starts out with established goals for sustainability and LEED certification. While this project did not start with established sustainability goals, the team worked together to achieve the desired level of certification.

Cost: The owner had proceeded with the project financing based on typical construction costs of the local area. This created an opportunity for the contractor and designer to demonstrate their innovation by completing the project on budget. Several decisions were made to increase the efficiency of the building systems while containing the costs of the construction so both budget and sustainability goals were maintained.

Team: The delivery team was made up of a designer with a passion for sustainability but no real-world LEED experience. The owner, who was very committed to the project, saw it as more than just building a building. This project was a part of a legacy the owner was leaving to family members who would continue to operate the family business. The contractor had both experience and success with other LEED buildings. The LEED consultant had worked with the majority of the team on past projects. The one thing that all members of the team had in common was a passion for the project. They worked together, always looking for opportunities to bring innovative ideas to the project. This team spirit enabled them to start the project with a LEED goal of Silver and complete the project by achieving Gold.

PROJECT 4

Project type: Institutional
Project size: 250,000 square feet
Project delivery: Design-build/Design-bid-build
Project owner: Public
LEED certification: LEED-NCv2.1 Gold

Introduction

In 2003, the community voted to proceed with a referendum of $29 million to deconstruct an existing facility and build a new school that would serve 650 students and provide an array of services to the community. The amenities would include a year-round exercise facility, a performance theater, and meeting rooms for community events. The new school would also provide much needed offices for the school district. This region had a long tradition of being close to the land.

Thus, the community endorsed the vision to develop a sustainable school. In response to this support, the decision was made to pursue LEED certification. The project emphasized connectivity to the surrounding environment through expansive daylighting and views from classrooms, offices, and the commons.

The team faced several major challenges early in the process:

- Schedule: Working through the winter of 2005–2006, the new school had to be ready for the first day of classes on September 5, 2006.
- Definition of the site boundary: The project included not only the new school building, but the redevelopment of some of the playing fields and the long-term rehabilitation and preservation of substantial acreage on-site. The over all campus included an adjacent K–8 school and playing fields that were not redeveloped. This presented both site design challenges and a rather unique project boundary.
- Proximity of site: The new school had to be built around and very close to the existing school, which could not be deconstructed until the end of the 2005–2006 academic year.
- Weather conditions: The area has a very long, cold winter and construction had to be planned around the weather conditions.

Scope

The 250,000-square-foot LEED Gold school consists of the following:

- Education wing including extensive science, technology, and IT classrooms, laboratories, shops, student guidance, a library, and a green house
- A 650-seat performance auditorium including an orchestra pit and stage
- Central administration offices that support the entire district
- A commons area—serving as the main entry, gathering place, and dining area for the school—designed to welcome students, families, community users, and guests to the school
- A field house including four basketball/volleyball competition courts, a six-lane track, and pits for other track and field events, with retractable seating available for 2,200 people
- Playing fields including a remodeled football field and outdoor track, and new baseball/softball diamonds
- Native restoration areas, some of which serve as an outdoor biology laboratory

Project

Sustainable Sites

The challenge of working with this expansive site and the need to deconstruct the old school was a tremendous challenge. However, with every challenge comes opportunity. Because this phase of the complex expansion was to be constructed on a previously developed site, much of the infrastructure was existing. Many of the natural areas were defined through the district's long-term commitment to the community. Several strategies were included into the design to help capture credits defined within Sustainable Sites. Bicycle storage racks were placed within 200 feet of the front entrance. The field house and fitness areas with locker rooms and showers were incorporated into the building design as an amenity for all building users. All of the areas along the northern boundary, the northeast corner, and a section surrounding a retention pond are either restored or preserved, including some old-growth forest, as a result of a long-term board commitment to protect open space and limit the development footprint.

All areas affected by the construction process were well protected from sedimentation and soil erosion during construction and continue to be protected by the owner during ongoing operations. An extensive stormwater retention effort is focused on two large retention ponds along with extensive native vegetation. The local department of natural resources has one of the nation's most stringent sets of requirements related to stormwater, resulting in no increase from predevelopment discharge rate and quantity as compared to postdevelopment. A specific plant species list was utilized and planted around the northern retention pond and other restoration areas for filtration of phosphorous and suspended solids. Because of the far northern climate, the desire to melt snow and ice on paved surfaces, and through detailed energy simulation of the building, the team made a decision not to pursue the heat island credits. In this environment, the limited heat island effects that exist are advantageous. This building uses less energy by incorporating a black roof rather than a white roof. The site photometric study indicates the use of full cutoff light fixtures throughout the site to reduce light pollution.

Water Efficiency

The use of native and adapted plant species allowed the team to eliminate a permanent irrigation system from the site design. All grass and plant species present on-site are drought-resistant, which allows them to survive without permanent irrigation systems. The district decided to use waterless urinals, dual-flush toilets, and low-flow fixtures to achieve a substantial water reduction that is estimated to save the school district over $6,000 per year.

Energy and Atmosphere

The district was keenly interested in reducing its energy bills. This is a very cold climatic zone and yet it can have some hot, humid periods in the summer. The school was designed with the guidance of extensive energy modeling, with the final design achieving a 46 percent energy cost savings. The lighting power densities were minimized and there are stepped daylighting controls in most classrooms. There is extensive use of motion sensors in the school that control both lighting and HVAC operation. After discussions with the district, the choice was made to use both fundamental and enhanced building commissioning. The ventilation requirements needed in the field house and the auditorium areas are controlled with CO_2 sensors.

Materials and Resources

The citizens of this area have a strong conservation ethic. Part of this derives from the hard life of the early settlers at around the turn of the twentieth century. The team set out with an aggressive program of local sourcing and recycling. This focus paid off with over 50 percent of materials being sourced from regional manufacturers and over 80 percent of construction waste diverted from landfills. Care was taken in selecting low-VOC materials, and wood, cardboard, metal, and concrete were recycled to the fullest extent possible.

Indoor Environmental Quality

The district made a commitment to provide a high standard of indoor air quality and comfort. A Construction Indoor Air Quality Plan was put in place and adhered to during construction. This extensive CIAQ plan was successfully implemented with the support of all contractors working on site. Careful attention was given to protecting HVAC ductwork and other components before and after installation. A building flush-out was completed prior to occupancy.

Innovation in Design

Education and Outreach: The project incorporates an extensive education plan, consisting of two initiatives, Energy Education and Field Education and Ecology. The Energy Education program integrates curriculum, training, and monitoring tools to make the school building an ongoing living laboratory. The second education initiative focuses on outdoor education. It involves the restoration of natural areas on the site and the use of those natural areas as a permanent laboratory.

Exemplary Performance: Innovation in Design credits were achieved for the project's exemplary performance in both MRc4: Recycled Content and MRc5: Regional Materials.

Green Cleaning Program: Another innovation credit was achieved for the adoption of a green cleaning management program.

Lessons Learned

Team: The owner (local school board) made a strong commitment to the community when they made the decision to pursue LEED certification for this project. The design-build firm started working on this project during the public referendum stage and supported and educated the members of the school board during the early planning phase of the project. The design-builder had "in-house" design capabilities as well as a strong commitment to sustainability with demonstrated experience with LEED certified buildings. Even with the level of commitment and experience, this team made the decision to hire a LEED consultant to assist with the overall strategy and project documentation that would be needed for final certification of the building.

Cost: This was a public project funded through a referendum passed by the people of the community. The school board had a mandate to be responsible with the money spent on this project. Since this was a referendum, the cost of the project was established before final construction documents had been created. This condition forced the designers working for the design-build contractor to be acutely aware of the cost of their design without forfeiting the sustainable features planned for the building.

LEED: The building design and construction went very smoothly. There were some difficulties, but less than most typical projects. One issue that was a persistent problem for the owner and the rest of the team was an individual who lived and worked in the community who was upset that his firm had not been chosen to be a member of the design team at the time the referendum was passed. This individual had made many comments at the various public school board meetings and had been disruptive in a select few town hall–style meetings. With the exception of this distraction, the design and build process was fairly uneventful. The project was completed on time and within budget, and it achieved the level of LEED certification anticipated by the owner.

LEED Update: This project was certified under LEED for New Construction Version 2.1. At the time that this project was certified, the obligations that go along with the Minimum Program Requirements created with LEED Version 3 did not exist. Owners of projects at that time did not have the risk of project decertification.

Years after the project was certified, the project team was notified by USGBC that they had received a written complaint making accusations that the building design did not achieve certain prerequisites and credit points. USGBC took action based on this written complaint to launch an investigation and informed the project team that the result of this investigation could include the building's decertification. However, after months of research and analysis, during which the project team had to produce and provide revised and additional project documentation, USGBC upheld the project's Gold level certification. This turn of events was completely unprecedented at the time. There was no indication that USGBC had ever taken this kind of action, nor was anyone aware that the process of investigation and possible decertification could take place on projects certified under rating systems other than LEED 2009.

PROJECT 5

Project type: Commercial building

Project size: 45,000 square feet

Project delivery: CM/GC negotiated delivery

Project owner: Private

LEED certification: LEED-CIv2.0 Silver

Introduction

The project was a tenant fit out of an existing core and shell building that had never had a tenant. The location of the space was inside one of the buildings in a multiple-unit complex. At the time of acquisition the complex included a manufacturing facility and related support buildings. The complex also included a "shell" building that had been intended for a new administrative office by the previous owner. After several years of operation in this complex, the owner made the decision to complete the tenant finish portion of this existing building. Shortly after the start of design the decision was made to pursue certification under the LEED-CI program. The general contracting/construction management firm, who had been awarded the project, hired a sustainability consultant to work with the architect of record to complete the design. Mechanical, electrical, and plumbing were to be delivered under a design-build-delivery process. A critical component in the selection of all contractors was the desire to have this portion of the facility designed and constructed as a LEED-CI certified space.

Work on the integrated design began immediately after the official notification to proceed. The team of owner, architects, engineers, construction manager, and representatives of the building occupants worked together to develop the final build solution for the project. The expanded team worked together throughout the procurement phase of the project integrating design concepts and sustainable strategies before construction began. Some of the major challenges facing the team included:

- Definition of the site boundary: Prior to the start of the project the existing complex supported a functioning manufacturing facility. During the time of the tenant fit-out, construction of the central utility complex and other ancillary buildings had begun but was not a part of this scope of work.
- Separation of the teams' scopes of work and unrelated contractors working in and around the space included under this contract.
- Existing infrastructure: For the most part all of the utilities needed in the building (main electrical distribution and HVAC equipment) existed prior to the start of the project. No concern for the LEED requirements had been made at the time of purchase and installation of this equipment.
- Completion of the space without interruptions to the manufacturing process.
- The scope of work was to design and construct the office space for occupants who would support the manufacturing processes conducted in the existing facility.
- Products manufactured in the existing facility are regulated by the Food and Drug Administration. Air quality and purity had to be controlled in order to guarantee purity of finished product. Contaminants from the construction process could not be allowed to comingle with any of the intake air supplying the manufacturing process.

Scope

At the time of the contractor's involvement in this project, construction of a chiller building was already progressing under the direction of a different contract. The contractor's scope of work requiring LEED-CI certification consisted of the following:

- Administration space: This portion of the complex housed the administrative functions supporting the manufacturing complex.
- No process equipment, automation, conveyors, central utilities equipment, or manufacturing process were included in the contractor's scope of work. The related scope of the project submitted for validation by USGBC was for the completion of the office space only.

Project

Another challenge for the team was working on a site where other general contractors were in the process of constructing other buildings that did not require LEED certification. The contractor's responsibility was for work required for the tenant finishes portion of the existing "shell" building. It was imperative to define where the scope of the other general contractors stopped and where this project team's scope started to consistently apply the strategies that went along with the requirement of LEED-CI certification.

Sustainable Sites

Several strategies were incorporated into the design to help capture credits defined within Sustainable Sites. Bicycle storage racks were placed within 200 feet of the front entrance of the building. Locker rooms and showers were incorporated into the building design as an amenity for the employees. The previous owner of this building was fortunately concerned about heat island effects, as evidenced by an existing high-albedo roofing material installed on the building. The parking requirements were adjusted to accommodate fewer cars and preferred parking for carpool vehicles.

Water Efficiency

The team worked with the local code officials to satisfy their concerns resulting in their approval of waterless urinals and low-flow fixtures to achieve water reductions.

Energy and Atmosphere

The owner believed in extensive commissioning for all building components. The result of the commissioning effort was a thorough inspection and functional test of each piece of equipment installed in this project. The owner's commitment to environmental stewardship allowed for the omission of CFC-based HVAC&R equipment from the design used on the project. The ventilation requirements needed in the manufacturing spaces of the buildings challenged the energy optimization of the building systems; nevertheless, the project was able to capture all energy optimization credit points.

Materials and Resources

The look and feel of the tenant spaces supported the intent of the Materials and Resources section of the rating system. The selection of the building components and finishes added to both recycled content and the use of local material suppliers.

The team sourced a local recycling vendor for all of the construction waste generated throughout the project. To the fullest extent possible, construction and finish materials were recycled.

Indoor Environmental Quality

The owner made a commitment to the employees to provide a high standard of workplace health and safety. As mentioned, the manufacturing processes were not included in the scope of this certification. However, the design of the buildings took the manufacturing process into account. The Construction Indoor Air Quality Program put in place during construction went beyond the suggestions of SMACNA by incorporating a biological pollution prevention protocol with the best practice guidelines. This extensive CIAQ plan was successfully implemented with the support of all contractors working on-site. The efforts made by the team were validated through indoor air quality testing before occupancy. The results of these tests validated the success of both the CIAQ management plan during construction and the efforts of the team's low-emitting strategy to keep off-gassing materials out of the building.

Innovation in Design

The magnitude of this project combined with the experience and talent possessed by the project team encouraged innovations in all they did.

Education and Outreach: The educational process started at the very first partnering session in which everyone on the extended design team was introduced to the LEED system. A symbol of the team's commitment to certification in the form of a project charter hung in all of the construction site trailers. A series of charrettes was conducted to further integrate the systems approach to the design of the buildings. The educational initiative continued with a formal educational program instituted by the owner.

Exemplary Performance: The constant attention to specifying and procuring materials allowed the team to surpass the intended goals for both MRc4: Recycled Content and MRc5: Regional Materials.

Lessons Learned

This project did not start out as a green project. When the design and planning for this project began there was no consideration or goal for the tenant improvements to be certified by USGBC. The contractor saw an opportunity when they realized that the overall environmental goals stated by the client aligned with the considerations of the LEED-CI rating system. Before construction began, the contractor arranged a tour of a LEED certified facility nearby the site. At the conclusion of the tour, the owner was very interested in exploring the possibility of pursuing LEED certification. The contractor worked with the estimating team and found ways to fund the effort under the original GMP budget. This information triggered the owner to seek certification of this space.

Because the design had already begun, the sustainability consultant was required to review the existing documents and identify any products or design aspects that were not compliant with the LEED requirements. They also assembled a manual to aid the trade contractors with the identification of the processes and products that would be required during the construction phase. The team also discovered that there were processes in place that supported the overall sustainability strategies for the project. The owner required commissioning on all process equipment installed at any of their facilities. Because of the owner's familiarity with the commissioning process, it was easy to incorporate that protocol for the equipment start-up in this space. The tenant fit-out work in the scope of this contract was in a building adjacent to an existing manufacturing facility. The air quality requirements of the existing facility restricted the construction team from using the permanent air handling equipment during construction. This requirement supported the CIAQ LEED credit without additional cost to the owner.

PROJECT 6

Project type: Commercial building
Project size: 9,400 square feet
Project delivery: CM/GC negotiated integrated delivery
Project owner: Private–Public entity leaser
LEED certification: LEED-NCv2.2 Silver

Introduction

The developers of this building saw an opportunity to demonstrate their commitment to environmental concerns by investing in the local community and providing a sustainable solution to the need for new lease office space. They assembled a team of professionals to assist them in making the project a reality. The developers began to work with architects on the initial conceptual design for the building. As the conceptual work was underway, the partners engaged a sustainability consultant and general contractor to work with the team at this early stage. The developers made a commitment to sustainable design and construction and to demonstrate this commitment, began the process of seeking to LEED certify this project.

The building and property is ideally located near major highways, while also providing ready access to the local community. The building's location, combined with the passion of the development partners, provided a platform to support both a need for this new office as well as a commitment to demonstrate an alternative approach to real estate development not widely seen in this particular marketplace.

Scope

The approximately 9,400-square-foot building incorporates the following:

- Reception/waiting area and guard desk
- Front-end interviewing (FEI) area and private interview rooms
- Closed and open office space
- Multipurpose room and interactive video-training (IVT) area with operable partition
- File, storage, computer server, and other support areas

Project

Sustainable Sites

The development team chose a suitable site for the project and the team worked diligently to limit the amount of site disturbance to the existing property. Green, open space, although not required by local zoning ordinance, was incorporated for more than 35 percent of the project's site area. The team carefully specified and installed a white membrane roofing material to decrease the heat island effects to the surrounding area. To promote alternative means of transportation, preferred parking was provided for low-emitting and fuel-efficient vehicles.

Water Efficiency

Water efficiency in the new building was a primary concern for the project team. The team worked with a landscape designer to develop a strategy to reduce the amount of potable water needed for irrigation purposes. In the end, several strategies were combined to realize this goal, including the incorporation of native and adapted plantings, mulch beds, drought-tolerant seed mixes, and a high-efficiency irrigation system. Water-efficient flush and flow fixtures were also specified and installed in the project, including the following choices:

- Dual-flush water closets
- Water-free urinal in one male restroom
- Low-flow lavatory and kitchen faucets

Energy and Atmosphere

The team worked to design a highly efficient envelope, while remaining within a conventional budget. The team utilized an energy model to help provide information about the energy efficiency of the building. The commissioning process implemented by the team ensured the building's systems were functioning optimally and as designed. Refrigerants were carefully chosen with regard to their ozone-depleting and global warming potentials to allow for achievement of both Fundamental and Enhanced Refrigerant Management (EAp3 and EAc4).

Materials and Resources

Recycling, reuse, and regionally sourced materials were a part of the project team's goals. Nearly 90 percent of the construction and demolition waste was carefully diverted from the landfill by way of recycling centers and reuse. Concrete, asphalt, cardboard, paper, and scrap wood were recycled. Recycled materials were found in many of the products specified and installed in the building, including insulation, steel, metal wall panels, and doorframes, as well as many of the finishes. Regional products were also highly valued by the team and over 40 percent of the construction materials were sourced and extracted within a 500-mile radius of the site.

Indoor Environmental Quality

The design and construction team focused on providing the future building users and occupants with exceptional indoor environmental quality. The ventilation system was designed to incorporate an outdoor air delivery monitoring system as well as an increased ventilation rate over the minimum required by ASHRAE. The incorporation of high-performance glazing allowed for the provision of views to the outdoors and a comfortable level of natural daylight for the building's occupants while having a positive effect on the energy efficiency of the building. All of the contractors working on-site followed a stringent no/low-emitting VOC policy and Construction Indoor Air Quality Management program during construction. Only no/low-emitting adhesives, sealants, paints, coatings, carpet systems, and composite woods were utilized by the team. The project team also scrutinized possible sources of indoor chemicals and pollutants, designing and building the project to minimize these contaminants. Thermal comfort for the future occupants was of primary importance to the team. To verify that the steps taken to optimize thermal comfort have been successful, the owners will utilize a survey of the occupants within eighteen months of move-in, as well as subsequent and appropriate corrective action should more than 20 percent show dissatisfaction.

Innovation

Education and Outreach: Educational information about the building was incorporated into signage explaining the sustainable features of the facility and the building's managers invite all interested groups to come and learn about sustainability through building tours.

Green Cleaning: To preserve the exceptional indoor air quality achieved during design and construction, the owners committed to the inclusion of a green cleaning management program that addresses both cleaning products and procedures.

Exemplary Performance: Additional innovation credits were achieved through the project's exemplary performance in the incorporation of Recycled Content (MRc4) and Regional Materials (MRc5).

Lessons Learned

Team: The owner/developer of this project was required by the tenant agreement of the lease to furnish a LEED certified space at a Silver level. They made a prudent decision when hiring a team that could work together for the project. Many members of the team did not have experience with the LEED process so a sustainability consultant was added to the team to assist in accelerating them through the learning curve that is associated with most projects. This allowed for the needs of the discipline engineers to support the aesthetic desires of the architect and the owner.

Cost: The owner of the building was no stranger when it came to the topic of cost or time required to deliver this type of project. In the past they had built other facilities that were very similar to these buildings and had a high expectation that the team would complete the projects on time and within budget. While the owner had experience with constructing facilities such as this, it was their first LEED building. The delivery team completed the project on time, to the LEED certification level desired by the owner and at the owner's traditional construction budget.

LEED: To a casual observer this building does not stand out or look that different from any other office building in the local area. The building was designed and constructed with many of the same materials you might find in any other building. The biggest difference in the design and construction of the building was the attention to detail paid when specifying, procuring, and installing the materials that came together as the finished project. When the project was submitted for review by USGBC, the comments returned by the reviewers of the project were very ordinary in nature and responses were easily formulated by the team. This is not always the case. Every project is different and reviewers are human. They have a set of guidelines that are used when reviewing the submitted information. It is important to remember that human beings are performing the documentation review. Equally important is to remember that there are several people who are contracted by USGBC to perform these reviews, and while they attempt to be impartial and objective in their reviews, each person may interpret the provided information differently. Just because the project seems to be very straightforward and the documentation that is associated with a LEED project submission is brought together with relative ease does not automatically mean that a team will receive an "easy" review. Again, this proves that no two projects are the same!

PROJECT 7

Project type: Commercial building

Project size: 24,000 square feet

Project delivery: CM/GC negotiated integrated delivery

Project owner: Private—Private entity leaser

LEED certification: LEED-CIv2.0 Gold

Introduction

This project is a tenant fit-out of a core and shell building. The developers of the business center in which the tenant fit-out is located demonstrated their commitment to environmental concerns by investing in the local community and purchasing several existing parcels of land with an existing manufacturing building on site. The building is located in what some would call an industrial area of the local county. The building was originally constructed in the 1950s as a manufacturing facility for a local company. Through the many years of the building's life, it functioned as a manufacturing and distribution warehouse prior to its purchase by the developer.

While the building was in adequate condition for medium to heavy manufacturing, it would require extensive renovation for its future intended use as speculative office space. The surrounding parcels sat unused and neglected along with the main building.

The business center partners saw something in this parcel that other developers had likely overlooked. They saw a unique chance to change the face of a neglected lot. They learned that through the renovation of the existing building, the addition of at least one building on the property and possibly another, the development company could communicate their mission and support the community surrounding the project. The building itself had a second life in it and could likely house up to three tenant companies when finished. The overall site had the potential to increase the density of an interior parcel of a prior development, allowing the team to avoid developing in the suburban areas that most developers tend to focus on.

The partners began to assemble a team of professionals to assist them in making the project a reality. The architect began to work with a sustainability consultant on the initial conceptual design for the building. As the conceptual work was underway, the partners engaged a local design-build contractor to work with the team. While the team worked to renovate the existing building under LEED for Core and Shell guidelines, the developers sought out a company to occupy the soon-to-be renovated green space. They quickly found a tenant and the office space at the business center would become their perfect fit.

The lessee chose the site for a variety of reasons. First, the parent company of this subsidiary had a corporate-wide commitment to social and environmental responsibility. The company is in the business of managing energy by developing technologies that enable an efficient use of natural resources, thereby reducing carbon emissions. Another reason the site was chosen was because of the parcel's location. The company's previous location was a stone's throw away from the new facility, so employees would not be forced to increase their commute time. The property is ideally located near a major transportation route that serves as a connector to other major highways and the local airport. Ultimately, the strongest motivator behind the decision to move into the facility was its new life as a "green" building. No division of its parent company had ever relocated to a facility such as this and it provided the opportunity to become a leader.

The parent company's ultimate mission of managing energy better and their goal of environmental protection went hand in hand with moving into a green building when the need to relocate arose. The company continually strives for constant improvement and innovative thinking, so why shouldn't their design team be held to the same standards?

The building was completed, occupancy occurred in summer of 2008, and the project became the first LEED certified tenant fit-out in the city where it is located.

The team faced several major challenges in the process of construction of the new tenant fit-out:

- Because certain rooms and portions of the building are used for light manufacturing and detailed assembly, and some areas are commercial office space, there are different conditioning and lighting needs for the space.
- The tenants had specific requirements for the space but had to stay within their budget while incorporating their sustainable solutions.

Scope

The approximately 24,000-square-foot tenant fit-out space incorporates the following concepts:

- Commercial office space with open office areas, conference rooms and employee amenities
- Light manufacturing, detailed assembly and warehouse space for meter production and storage

Project

Sustainable Sites

The team worked to reduce the amount of parking to less than that required by local zoning ordinances and still meet the needs of the tenant. The property is also located within a quarter mile of two bus lines. The office is part of a new business center, a redevelopment project utilizing a previous manufacturing facility to create an urban infill, state-of-the art bustling business center to increase commercial density in the interior of the metropolitan area.

Water Efficiency

Water efficiency in the project was important to the tenants and the development team. Low-flow fixtures were chosen and installed. Additionally, rainwater is captured and stored in an underground tank for use in site irrigation.

Energy and Atmosphere

The facility was designed with increased insulation values, high-performance low-e glazing, and mechanical efficiency while sticking to a conventional budget. The goal was to relocate to an energy-efficient space that housed both commercial office space and a light manufacturing/detailed assembly area. The commissioning process allowed for the owners to verify that their facilities were operating as designed. The facility is designed for separate solar exposures to ensure maximum energy efficiency. The facility's mechanical equipment is designed to meet the prerequisite of no CFC-based refrigerants (EAp3). The mechanical equipment is also designed to recognize occupied and unoccupied modes for peak efficiency and ultimate utility savings, while utilizing an underfloor air distribution system.

Materials and Resources

Recycling, building reuse, and regionally sourced materials were incorporated into the project. The interior finishes portray a multitude of environmentally friendly materials. The flooring consists of utilizing the already present concrete floor and sealing it in heavy-use areas and installing a high recycled content, low-emitting carpet in the office areas. During construction, the crew carefully recycled and salvaged materials in order to divert construction and demolition waste from local landfills. The break room has specific areas for collection and storage of recyclables. The tenant's management team has also identified various other opportunities for recycling in the day-to-day operations and light manufacturing and is making sure that as little waste leaves the site as possible moving forward.

Indoor Environmental Quality

The tenant requested that the office areas be full of natural daylighting so the design team found ways to increase the vision glass and added skylights to the existing roof for maximum daylighting opportunities. The design team also made sure to specify materials that were low-emitting and occupant safe. The construction team and subcontractors followed a strict Construction Indoor Air Quality Management program on the site, further safeguarding the future tenant occupants. Operable windows were also installed so occupants can have the opportunity to enhance their indoor space with fresh, outside air.

Innovation in Design

This project had a great starting point to begin its journey toward a "green" facility and the team took that process to heart throughout the project's entire timeline. In the end, several LEED credit thresholds were exceeded and the team achieved all possible Innovation in Design points, including:

- Exemplary Performance, EAc4: Green Power
- Exemplary Performance, MRc6: Rapidly Renewable Materials
- Education and Outreach Program
- Green Cleaning Management Plan

Lessons Learned

Integrated delivery can have different meanings and different outcomes depending on the team. In this case the team used an integrated approach in that the designers, contractor, and developer were involved in the project from the very start. However, the LEED process was not integrated into all of the decisions.

Because the team had worked together on numerous projects in the past, little information was assembled in the form of drawings and specifications. Individual members of the delivery team acknowledged their responsibilities and during the planning stages of the project, they confirmed that they understood what was required to be in the design. Problems started to surface during the delivery of the project. The contractor was accustomed to a traditional delivery process. The size of the firm and the projects that they were comfortable with did not dictate having robust or sophisticated processes in place. They typically worked with the same subcontractors on every project. The accumulated familiarity with team members worked against them when completing this project. Site audits during the construction phase indicated that the vast majority of workers did not know that they were working on a LEED project. Certain materials purchased by the site office did not comply with the LEED requirements. Paperwork and documentation was almost nonexistent. The schedule was dictated by availability of manpower instead of a contractual end date.

Because the contractors working on-site did not document procurement of materials throughout construction, additional time and effort was needed to locate the information needed to demonstrate compliance with the LEED requirements. Much of the material that was used on this project was purchased in bulk rather than specific to the job. Quantity surveys of the as-built condition were used in combination with "per piece" pricing indicated on mixed material invoices. Tickets from the local recycler and waste disposal companies did not reference this specific project. Materials salvaged from other sites and used in this project were not documented. Assembling the documentation necessary for the project submission became a forensic exercise.

Additional difficulties were encountered when documenting many of the design-related credits. When the design team was asked to furnish their information, much of the detail necessary to complete the submission was lacking.

Even though they had acknowledged that they understood the requirements during the design phase, they actually did not understand the difference between details required for permitting and the LEED requirements. Drawings had to be created and documents had to be produced in order to demonstrate compliance with certain credits.

The project was completed. The tenant is very happy with the space. The developer now has a tenant under a long-term lease agreement. There is another LEED certified project in the local community. However, the project team was unable to document all of the credit points they had originally thought they were going to achieve, and gaining the points they did achieve took time and effort that was not calculated at the start of the project.

PROJECT 8

Project type: Institutional building
Project size: 190,000 square feet
Project delivery: CMA/GC hard bid
Project owner: Public/community
LEED certification: LEED-Schools v2007 Gold

Introduction

Faced with an out-of-date school building and expanding enrolment, this school district found itself asking a hard question. Do we renovate the existing building or look to relocate the school and build new? As the school embarked on a process to examine all of the available options, they started to ask another question: Why wouldn't a school district faced with educating tomorrow's leaders practice what they preach? After careful deliberation, the decision was made to build a new school in a more appropriate location serving more of the community—both in student proximity and shared space with the community. The new location is in a suburb of a major metropolitan area, close to major highways and existing community infrastructure. The design team realized that they were creating a symbiotic, inclusive structure that serves students and the community.

The school began to work with the architects on the initial conceptual design, which suggested smarter square footage for the school's programming needs, as opposed to merely adding bigger spaces. As the conceptual work was underway, the team was expanded to include a sustainability consultant and a construction manager to work with the team.

Scope

The 190,000-square-foot building incorporates the following:

- Inclusive stormwater plan on 22 acres including bioswales and permeable paving where possible
- Divided building functions separating public and private spaces that contribute to energy efficiency and safe community usage during nonschool hours
- Native vegetation and a partial green roof
- Classrooms never lacking in natural daylight and less-used spaces on the interior (music areas most notably) designed with rooftop monitors to bring in the light the perimeter cannot provide
- Energy-efficient design with the plug-and-play mentality for future inclusion of renewable energy

Project

Sustainable Sites

The school district and design team chose a suitable site for the project and ultimately succeeded in limiting the commute time for most of the students. The team carefully specified and installed a white membrane roofing material to decrease the heat island effects to the surrounding area and included a small amount of green roof located over the second-floor administrative offices. To promote alternative means of transportation, preferred parking was provided for low-emitting and fuel-efficient vehicles in not one but two different parking lots on the site to serve both the playing fields and the new facility. Bioswales and other best management practices were integrated in the north and south portions of the site. Demonstrating a good neighbor policy, the site accepts some stormwater from a neighboring community property.

Water Efficiency

Water efficiency in the new building was just one concern for the project team. The team worked with a landscape designer to incorporate native landscaping and adapted plantings throughout the entire site. Water-efficient flush/flow fixtures in the restroom and school's cafeteria were also specified and installed, including the following choices:

- Dual-flush water closets
- Low-flow lavatory faucets
- Low-flow kitchen faucets and prerinse valves

Energy and Atmosphere

The team used an energy model to help provide information about the energy efficiency of the building. A careful balance between glass to skin was struck to maximize the building envelope efficiency. Stone cladding was selected for external walls enhancing the visual aspect and providing a high insulation value. A very high performing "super" glass used in conjunction with fixed shading devices rounded off the triple-feature envelope. Operating differences in a school guided the designers to zone areas of the building appropriately for school or community use. The commissioning process implemented by the team ensured the building's systems were designed per the school districts requirements before the construction documents were issued. The requirements of fundamental commissioning were fulfilled before occupancy and enhanced commissioning activities will conclude prior to the end of the warranty period. Refrigerants were carefully chosen with regard to their ozone-depleting and global warming potentials to allow for achievement of both Fundamental and Enhanced Refrigerant Management (EAp3/EAc4).

Materials and Resources

Over 82 percent of the construction and demolition waste was carefully diverted from the landfill by way of recycling centers. Concrete, asphalt, cardboard, paper, and scrap wood were recycled. Recycled materials were found in many of the products specified and installed in the building including insulation, steel, metal wall panels, and doorframes, as well as many of the finishes resulting in over 34 percent recycled content of building materials. Regional products were also highly valued by the team and the design team chose to highlight regional products in the design such as the prairie stone on the exterior. Over 20 percent of the construction materials were sourced and extracted within a 500-mile radius of the site area.

Indoor Environmental Quality

The design and construction team focused on providing the school's students, administration, staff, and community visitors with exceptional indoor environmental quality. The ventilation system was designed to incorporate an outdoor air delivery monitoring system. Views are abundant in the space bringing the outdoors "in." All of the contractors working on site followed a stringent no/low-emitting VOC policy and Construction Indoor Air Quality Management program during construction. Only no/low-emitting adhesives, sealants, paints, coatings, carpet systems, and composite woods were utilized by the team. Thermal comfort for the future occupants was of primary importance to the team. To verify thermal comfort, the owners will utilize a survey of the occupants within 18 months of move-in, and take appropriate corrective action should more than 20 percent show dissatisfaction. The team is certain the indoor environmental quality provided for the school's staff, teachers, students, and visitors is the freshest and healthiest possible. Additionally, the district has adopted a mold prevention protocol designed to prevent mold first and foremost in a variety of locations and scenarios.

Innovation in Design

Education and Outreach Program: Educational information about the building has been incorporated into signage explaining the sustainable features of the space and is incorporated into many areas of the curriculum as well.

Green Cleaning Program: As required by state law and in an effort to preserve the exceptional indoor air quality achieved during design and construction, the district is committed to the inclusion of a green cleaning management program that addresses both cleaning products and procedures.

Exemplary Performance: Additional innovation credits are sought through the project's exemplary performance in SSc5.2: Site Development—Maximize Open Space and MRc4: Recycled Content. The facility hopes to be a model for educational and community facilities for years to come.

Lessons Learned

The entire team put forth a genuine effort to complete this project. As with any project, LEED or non-LEED, weather can wreak havoc on a contractor's schedule. This project was no exception. Throughout the construction phase of the project, severe weather delayed critical activities. In the rush to complete certain areas of the building, the time scheduled for building flush-out had to be used to make up for time lost earlier in the construction phase. Even dedicated teams must at times choose between the requirements of the LEED rating system and the on-time completion of the project.

The owner had strict requirements for the durability and maintenance of the gymnasium floor. This requirement makes perfect sense from a facility management perspective, but did not have an exact fit with certain LEED protocols. The owner had specified a certain type and manufacturer for the gym floor. The manufacturer of this floor would warrant the product only if a specific floor sealer was used for floor finish. This particular sealer was not compliant with EQc4.1: Low-Emitting Materials—Adhesives and Sealants. The team wanted to fulfill the requirements of the owner and the LEED protocol, so a VOC budget was used to document compliance with the credit requirements. The budget methodology is allowed under the LEED rating system, but it can be a difficult process to document. In order for a team to successfully apply this method they must first collect VOC data on every adhesive and sealant used on the project. Then they must document the quantity of each of these products. A spreadsheet is then used to compile the data of VOC content, quantity of product used, and the permissible level of VOC for each product to create a budget. If the combined VOC levels of the design case scenario are below the budgeted allowable threshold levels, then the team has documented compliance with the credit.

Even a dedicated team must deal with requirements of the owner and the unpredictability of the weather.

PROJECT 9: BENEDICTINE WOMEN OF MADISON

Benedictine Women of Madison/Holy Wisdom Monastery

Project type: Ecumenical building

Project size: 34,000 square feet

Project delivery: Design-build

Project owner: Private

LEED certification: LEED-NCv2.2 Platinum

Introduction

A primary mission of the Benedictine Women of Madison is to work toward environmental solutions and to teach the importance of nature in religious and daily life. Their mission states that care for the earth is borne from their spirituality. The order believes that the earth is a gift to mankind and it must be preserved, maintained and restored at all costs. The order strives to use only what they need so that resources can be preserved for others, so it was natural they strove beyond conventional building practices when they realized that their old facility needed to be decommissioned and replaced.

The dilemma faced by the order was that their campus included an obsolete, energy-wasteful facility that had become a financial burden to operate. Preliminary estimates to renovate totaled several million dollars. After considerable study and consultation, the decision was made to replace the building with something smaller, built to the highest level of LEED certification and designed ultimately to achieve a "zero carbon footprint" through future renewable upgrades.

It was decided that the new building would be built close to the site of the decommissioned facility and overlooking one of the nearby lakes in the area. Right from the start, the owners turned to an architecture firm with experience in both religious architecture as well as sustainability. They tapped a sustainability consultant to provide additional support throughout the LEED process. In addition, the architect engaged a qualified mechanical, electrical, and plumbing designer. The architect also served as the construction manager ensuring continuity throughout the entire project.

With a dynamic team in place, the project's design started to take shape. The goal to have the building become certified by USGBC quickly sharpened the team's focus and design challenges became goals capable of being reached. Every member of the project team believed in the building and had a strong desire to find the full potential of this project: Platinum. The team found innovative ways to employ strategies that enhanced sustainability at little or no additional cost to construction. Through the combined design and construction knowledge of the team, and led by the vision of the order, the team achieved a Platinum level certification under the LEED for New Construction rating system, at 63 points, the highest LEED-NC Platinum rating in the United States to date.

Scope

The 34,000-square-foot, two-level building incorporates the following:

- Main facility, oratory, and smaller facility spaces for services and other group events
- Offices and meeting rooms for staff
- Dining areas for daily meals as well as special events
- New library and archive spaces
- Outdoor gathering spaces
- Accessible green roof on a portion of the building over the garage

Project

Sustainable Sites

The development team chose to build on the previously developed site where the facility once stood. The team worked diligently to limit the amount of site disturbance to the existing property. Though no green or open space was required by local zoning ordinance, the design incorporated open areas for close to 70 percent of the project's site area, much of which was restored to native prairie habitat. The team carefully specified and installed a white membrane roof, high-albedo paving surfaces, and a portion of permeable concrete to decrease the heat island effect on-site. To promote alternative means of transportation, preferred parking has been provided for low-emitting and fuel-efficient vehicles as well as for those who carpool to the site.

Water Efficiency

Water efficiency has always been a primary concern for the order. They currently maintain large prairie restorations and other gardens around the site. It was of utmost importance that any landscaping created through the course of the development of the new facility would not require any permanent irrigation from potable water. Water for use in the plant care room is collected in four rain barrels that capture stormwater off the monastery roof. Water-efficient flush and flow fixtures were also specified and installed in the project, including the following choices:

- 1.0-gallon-per-flush toilets
- Waterless urinals
- Low-flow lavatory and kitchen faucets

Energy and Atmosphere

The design of the mechanical system reflects the team's careful attention to energy efficiency. The facility uses a ground-source heat pump HVAC system featuring 39 wells installed under the parking lot. In addition, an initial phase of the photovoltaic (PV) renewable energy system has been installed providing about 13 percent of the estimated annual energy cost. As fundraising proceeds, the vision is to add additional PV to provide 100 percent of the energy cost on a net annual basis. This is a realistic goal given the projected low-energy usage of the building. The team worked to design a highly efficient envelope, while remaining within a conventional budget. Energy modeling software was used to help provide information about the energy efficiency of the building. The commissioning process implemented by a third party ensured that the building's systems were functioning optimally and as designed. In addition, a comprehensive measurement and verification program was instituted to provide meaningful data on the building's performance. Refrigerants were carefully chosen with regard to their ozone-depleting and global warming potentials to allow for achievement of both Fundamental and Enhanced Refrigerant Management (EAp3/EAc4).

Materials and Resources

Environmentally sensitive material choices were a part of the project team's core goals. Over 99 percent of the construction and demolition waste was carefully diverted from the landfill by way of recycling centers, reuse, and donations. Concrete, asphalt, cardboard, drywall, and scrap wood were recycled. In addition, nearly all of the building materials and finishes from the old facility were diverted from the landfill. Recycled materials were found in many of the products specified and installed in the building, including insulation, steel, concrete, and doors, as well as many of the finishes. Regional products were also highly valued by the team and close to 30 percent of the construction materials were sourced and extracted within a 500-mile radius of the site. Bamboo flooring and agrifiber board in the casework provided much of the rapidly renewable content within the project and over 50 percent of all new wood-based materials are FSC certified.

Indoor Environmental Quality

The design and construction team focused on providing the future building users and occupants with exceptional indoor environmental quality. The ventilation system was designed to incorporate an outdoor air delivery monitoring system. The incorporation of high-performance glazing allowed for the provision of views to the outdoors and a comfortable level of natural daylight for the building's occupants while having a positive effect on the energy efficiency of the building. All of the contractors working on site followed a stringent no/low-emitting VOC policy and Construction Indoor Air Quality Management program during construction. Only no/low-emitting adhesives, sealants, paints, coatings, carpet systems, and composite woods were utilized by the team. The project team also scrutinized possible sources of indoor chemicals and pollutants, designing and building the project to minimize these contaminants. Indoor air quality was validated by air quality testing. Thermal comfort as well as lighting control for the future occupants was of primary importance to the team. To verify that the steps taken to optimize thermal comfort have been successful, the owners will utilize a survey of the occupants within eighteen months of move-in, and take appropriate corrective action should more than 20 percent show dissatisfaction.

Innovation in Design

The one thing this project team had no shortage of was innovation.

Education and Outreach: The order invites all interested groups to come and learn about the building and sustainability. Educational information about the building has been incorporated into signage explaining the sustainable features of the space.

Green Cleaning Program: To preserve the exceptional indoor air quality achieved during design and construction, the owners are committed to the inclusion of a green cleaning management program that addresses both cleaning products and procedures.

Exemplary Performance: Additional innovation credits were achieved through the project's exemplary performance in water use reduction (WEc3) and inclusion of rapidly renewable materials (MRc6).

Lessons Learned

The design-build contractor working on this project had experience working on LEED projects. The familiarity with the LEED requirements helped in making decisions regarding other design members and trade contractors. Many of the LEED credit points rely on the contractor's ability to document the activities during construction. On this project, the design-build contractor had assigned one person at the beginning of the project to track the procurement of all materials used during the construction. This continuity made for quick work when assembling the submission for USGBC's review.

All of the contractors working on-site supported the LEED effort. Their combined efforts allowed for exemplary performance in diverting construction and demolition waste from the landfill. Workers used segregated waste containers for those materials that were accepted by the local recycling firm. Extra effort was noticed when workers found creative uses for some of the waste material that would not have been accepted by the recycler but could be used at individual homes for crafts and hobbies. The design team made extra effort to source materials from local vendors. Local material sourcing helped to gain both of the associated LEED credit points and sent a positive message to the community that this owner was truly interested in supporting the local economy.

The owner set the goals for the project at the very earliest stage of conceptual design. The owner wanted to demonstrate commitment to the community, to the environment, and to the world through the sustainable activities used to deliver this project. Energy efficiency, land stewardship, and water conservation efforts demonstrate a smaller footprint on the built environment. The use of low- or no-emitting materials, improved ventilation techniques, daylighting, and views to outdoor areas demonstrates to all building users that their well-being is important to this owner. Achieving a LEED Platinum certification with a higher accumulated score than any other LEED-NC building at or near the same cost as a conventional building of this type demonstrates to the world that if a team puts all its effort into innovative thinking, green buildings do not have to be more expensive than conventional construction.

▨ PROJECT 10

Project type: Commercial building
Project size: 57,200 square feet
Project delivery: Design-build
Project owner: Public
LEED certification: LEED-NCv2.2 Silver

Introduction

Through the joint efforts of the city manager and the economic development authority, the city developed a plan and secured the necessary funding for the design and construction of a much-needed new community health facility.

The building is ideally located near major highways, while also providing ready access to the local community. The city envisioned that the facility would serve as a catalyst in the rebirth of a declining area of the city. The building's location, combined with the passion and commitment of the city, provided a platform to support both a need for a new facility for the community as well as a demonstration of an alternative approach to the development of municipal facilities not widely seen in the local marketplace. With its team assembled, the owner set a goal for LEED certification of the building.

Scope

The facility was designed to house two community service departments and provides a variety of services for the community, including health screenings, immunizations, prenatal and pediatric services, family planning, senior services, and home health. The approximately 57,200-square-foot building incorporates the following:

- Reception/waiting area
- Services screening area and private interview rooms
- Examination, testing, and treatment areas
- Closed and open office space
- Conference, training, and multipurpose rooms
- File, storage, and other support areas

Project

Sustainable Sites

The development team chose a suitable site for the project, ensuring that the project would have exceptional connectivity with the surrounding community. Green, open space, although not required by local zoning ordinance, was incorporated for more than 21 percent of the project's site area. A retention basin was incorporated into the site's stormwater management design and also serves as an amenity feature for the building's visitors and occupants, complete with extensive walking trails. The team carefully specified and installed a white membrane roofing material to decrease the heat island effects to the surrounding area. To promote alternative means of transportation, bicycle storage and changing rooms are provided, as well as preferred parking for low-emitting and fuel-efficient vehicles.

Water Efficiency

Water efficiency in the new building was a primary concern for the project team. Water-efficient flush and flow fixtures were specified and installed in the project, including the following choices:

- Dual-flush water closets
- Water-free urinal in select male restrooms
- Ultra-low-flow lavatory and kitchen faucets
- Low-flow shower

Energy and Atmosphere

The team worked to design a highly efficient envelope, while remaining within a conventional budget and utilized the commissioning process to ensure the building's systems were functioning optimally and as designed. A detailed Measurement and Verification protocol was developed to ensure the building continues to operate at its peak efficiency.

Materials and Resources

Through a carefully implemented construction waste management plan, more than 90 percent of the construction and demolition waste was diverted from the local landfills by way of recycling centers and reuse. Concrete, wood, and metal were all separated and recycled. Recycled materials were found in many of the products specified and installed in the building including crushed concrete fill, insulation, steel, aluminum storefront panels, and metal doorframes, as well as many of the finishes, including gypsum panels, carpet, and ceiling tile. Regional products were also utilized by the team and over 30 percent of the construction materials were sourced and extracted within a 500-mile radius of the site. FSC certified wood was also used for the majority of the door core materials in the project.

Indoor Environmental Quality

The design and construction team focused on providing the future building users and occupants with exceptional indoor environmental quality. The ventilation system was designed to incorporate an outdoor air delivery monitoring system to ensure that levels of CO_2 in the building do not significantly vary from design parameters. All of the contractors working on site followed a stringent no/low-emitting VOC policy and Construction Indoor Air Quality Management program during construction. Only no/low-emitting adhesives, sealants, paints, coatings, carpet systems, and composite woods were utilized by the team. Thermal comfort for the future occupants was of primary importance to the team. To verify that the steps taken to optimize thermal comfort have been successful, the owners will conduct a survey of the occupants within eighteen months of move-in, and take appropriate corrective action should more than 20 percent show dissatisfaction.

Innovation in Design

Education and Outreach: The building's management team provides tours for all groups interested in the building and sustainability. Educational information about the building has been incorporated into signage explaining the sustainable features of the space.

Exemplary Performance: Through the selection of low-flow and efficient fixtures the team achieved exemplary performance with a greater than 41 percent reduction in potable water use (WEc3). Additionally, the project achieved more than 33 percent recycled content, allowing for achievement of another ID credit for MRc4.

Lessons Learned

Team: The owner of this project had made a decision to experiment with LEED certification for this building. The owner had never built a LEED building and used this opportunity to test a model that, if successful, would be used for all future projects within their control. They made a decision to utilize a design-build delivery model that placed the control of the design under the responsibility of the contractor building the project. Many members of the team did not have experience with the LEED process, so a sustainability consultant was added to the normal team to assist in accelerating the team through the learning curve that is associated with most projects. While the topic of LEED was new for most of the team, the definition of sustainable design was not. The discipline engineers worked to develop a design that supported the aesthetic desires of the architect and the budget driven by the owner.

Cost: The owner had not constructed a new building for many years but did have detailed knowledge of project costs and the time required to deliver this type of project. The design-build contractor was involved in the project at the very earliest stages, which allowed systematic budgets to be developed at every stage of design. The expectation that the team would complete the projects on time and within budget was managed through periodic budget reviews during the design phase. The delivery team completed this building on time, to the LEED certification level desired by the owner, and at the owner's traditional construction budget.

LEED: To a casual observer this building does not stand out or look very different from any other office building in the local area. The building was designed and constructed with many of the same materials found in any other building. The biggest difference in the design and construction of the building was the attention to detail paid when specifying, procuring, and installing the materials that came together as the finished project. When the project was submitted for review by USGBC, the comments received by the reviewers for the project were routine, allowing for a relatively simple supplemental submittal process. This is not always the case. Every project is different and reviewers are human, with set guidelines that are used to review the submitted information. It is important to remember that human beings are performing the documentation review. Equally important to remember is that there are several people who are contracted by USGBC to perform these reviews and while they attempt to be impartial and objective in their reviews, each person can interpret the provided information differently. Just because the project seems to be very straightforward and the documentation that is associated with a LEED project submission is brought together with relative ease, does not automatically mean that a team will receive an easy review. Again, this proves that no two projects are the same!

PROJECT 11

Project type: Educational building

Project size: 18,000 square feet renovation and 9,000 square feet addition

Project delivery: Design-bid-build

Project owner: Private

LEED certification: LEED-NCv2.2 Platinum

Introduction

When the school was faced with expanding enrollment, the school board and administration started asking some very difficult questions in an effort to examine all options on the table. One option was to update the current school, which is located in an old grocery store. Another option was to remodel and/or build on a recently donated parcel of land where an abandoned hardware shop and parking lot were situated. A third option was to build a small wing, adding classroom space and remodeling used spaces while updating the mechanical equipment. When all options were examined, the best choice emerged to build a new wing and remodel the majority of the existing facility. The addition would house a new library and classrooms for science, biology, physics, and chemistry. The school board made a commitment to sustainable design and construction early on when considering a new facility and knew that achieving LEED certification was the primary goal. They worked with a sustainability consultant, proving sustainability was of utmost importance and starting that process at the early conceptual design stage. The initial conceptual design for the building work was handed off to a professional urban developer who completed the team, adding an architect of record and remaining design team partners. The entire team was committed to the project and its eventual LEED certification.

Scope

The new addition and renovation incorporates the following:

- 18,000 square feet of existing renovation and mezzanine space
- Updated music room and computer lab
- New student common areas
- Complete overhaul of the HVAC system
- Addition of new skylights
- 9,000 square feet of a new construction
- Chemistry, biology, and physics labs
- Student work display area
- New library
- Fast-tracked schedule, including working during school vacations and night shifts, to complete the building in time for the 2009–2010 academic school year

Project

Sustainable Sites

The team worked diligently to limit the amount of site disturbance to the existing property. Some examples include:

- Permeable walkways and very limited hardscape
- Inclusive stormwater plan on the small site including bioswales, a rain garden planted by volunteers, and space for a future outdoor classroom
- Use of 100 percent concrete paving instead of asphalt to minimize the heat-island effect
- Designation of preferred parking for low-emitting/fuel-efficient vehicles

Water Efficiency

Water efficiency in the new facility was a primary concern for the project team. The team worked with a landscape designer initially. However, after seeing the landscape design and too many non-native plants in the mix, the chair of the school board decided to take on the landscape redesign as a personal mission. Professional advice was solicited on rain garden designs and a unique, site-specific solution emerged. Several strategies were combined to maximize stormwater capture, including the incorporation of native plantings in a large rain garden visible outside the science wing. Plumbing fixture selection was extremely important to the team and ultra-water-efficient flush and flow fixtures were also specified to maximize the project's overall water savings. Selections included the following:

- Dual-flush water closets
- Pint urinals
- Low-flow lavatory fixtures

Energy and Atmosphere

The team worked to design a highly efficient envelope for the new addition, while adding daylight to dark spaces such as the hallways and study areas where students naturally gravitate. Refrigerants were chosen with regard to their ozone-depleting and global warming potentials to allow for achievement of both Fundamental and Enhanced Refrigerant Management. A solar hot water system was installed to provide the majority of hot water in the addition.

Materials and Resources

Recycling, reuse, and regionally sourced materials were important to the team. Over 95 percent of the construction and demolition waste was carefully diverted from the landfill by way of recycling centers and reuse. Concrete, asphalt, cardboard, drywall, and scrap wood were recycled. In addition, old ceiling tile and other building finishes were donated to Habitat for Humanity and a local church and school. Recycled materials were found in many of the newly purchased products specified and installed in the building. Some examples include insulation, steel, metal wall panels, and concrete. Study carrels in the renovation were removed and reinstalled following construction, preserving materials as well as a favorite student hangout. Running the length of the new hallway is a bright, cheery non-PVC based, no-VOC resilient tile, which provides a healthier flooring alternative. Finally, one of the greenest parts of this project was the use of previously donated new carpet for the library. Not only did this save a large amount of material from the landfill, but it was budget friendly (free) and serendipitously Green Label Plus Certified.

Indoor Environmental Quality

The design and construction team focused on providing the students and staff with excellent indoor environmental quality. The ventilation system was designed to incorporate an outdoor air delivery monitoring system. The incorporation of high performance glazing allowed for the provision of views to the outdoors and a comfortable level of natural daylight for the building's occupants while having a positive effect on the energy efficiency of the building. All of the contractors working on site followed a stringent no/low-emitting VOC policy and Construction Indoor Air Quality Management program during construction. The project team also scrutinized possible sources of indoor chemicals and pollutants, designing and building the project to minimize these contaminants and testing afterward for compliance of strict indoor air standards. Indoor environmental quality provided for the office's staff, clients, and visitors is the freshest and healthiest possible, benefiting all who enter the doors at the school.

Innovation in Design

During the construction phase of the project, the school's weekly newsletter had updates on construction and also tidbits on greening the school. After construction was complete, the school continued to make sustainability part of the curriculum, making it an integral part of the school's culture. Prominently located at the main entrance, educational information about the building was incorporated into signage for all who enter to see. Real-time building monitoring data is shown on the flat panel in the front lobby. To preserve the exceptional indoor air quality achieved during design and construction, the owners are committed to the inclusion of a green cleaning management program that addresses both cleaning products and procedures. Through the team's careful planning and execution, additional innovation credits were awarded through the project's exemplary performance in the reduction of heat island effect, nonroof (SSc7.1), and construction waste management (MRc2).

Lessons Learned

The school had identified an immediate need for additional space in order to accommodate the student body. However, as is the case with most private institutions, the money to fund this capital project had to be raised before the construction could commence. This owner found that while time worked to their benefit in terms of evaluation of multiple design schemes, it worked against them in terms of team continuity and estimated cost of construction. Shortly after the architect who began the project finished with conceptual design, a professional development firm was hired to assist in the funding and management of the project. This addition to the team brought a change in architects and with that an entirely new design team. While it is true that changes made early in a project have a small cost impact to the construction costs, this change impacted the design costs significantly.

Changing the design team also altered the course of project delivery. In the early stages of project planning, the school board had intended to use a design-build philosophy for the construction of the project. The design-build process seemed to lend itself to the renovation portion of the project since there would most likely be unforeseen conditions not discovered until selective demolition could take place. However, the new design team insisted that a design-build delivery was inappropriate for the project and convinced the school board to use a traditional design-bid-build approach. The design-build philosophy could have created a situation where a "low-bid" contractor, looking only at the information contained in the contract documents, may have excluded many aspects of the project that were not clearly indicated on the drawings or in the specifications. Fortunately, there was one consistent member of the team who assisted in the dissemination of information throughout the project. Equally fortunate was that the contractor saw an opportunity to work on their first LEED project and decided to use it as a learning tool.

During the bid process the contractor worked very hard to understand everything that would be required of them and their subcontractors. They asked questions during the process and that knowledge resulted in a low price on bid day, and the confidence that they could successfully complete the project. The estimator worked with the sustainability consultant and the rest of the design team to include all of the material and possibly more important the processes required to document all of the LEED related credits. Project management was led by one of the contractor's top executives who wanted to learn firsthand what a LEED project was all about. He applied this newly acquired knowledge and instructed all personnel working on the project how important it was for them to support the sustainability effort through their work.

At the completion of the project, this effort paid off in the success of the project. The project was delivered on time and within budget, achieved safety goals, and succeeded in becoming LEED Platinum.

PROJECT 12: ALBERICI HEADQUARTERS

Project type: Commercial office building

Project size: 110,000 square adaptive reuse

Project delivery: Integrated delivery

Project owner: Private

LEED certification: LEED-NCv2.1 Platinum

Introduction

At the start of this project the owner purchased a previously developed industrial site for a new headquarters. The site of 14 acres included two buildings used by the previous owner. These buildings supported the packaging and distribution of metal goods. One building was a 50,000-square-foot three-story brick office building located north of the second structure. Building two was a 150,000-square-foot single-story manufacturing/distribution facility. The larger of the two structures was to be adaptively reused creating class "A" office space.

Chairman of the firm, John Alberici, provided the vision of adaptively reusing the manufacturing building to the highest levels of sustainability. As a third-generation construction professional he was well acquainted with the impact of the construction industry on the natural environment. He wrote:

> In 2002, when we decided to take a "green" approach to constructing our new corporate headquarters, an important question arose: just how green did we want to be?

After reviewing information on the U.S. Green Building Council's Leadership in Energy and Environmental Design (LEED®) certification program, we decided to set our sights on attaining the highest certification level offered—Platinum.

The decision to build a Platinum building wasn't difficult to make and wasn't made solely on the prospect of achieving notoriety for our company. Rather it was made for future employees . . . for those who aren't even born yet. We had to take the long view and think of their well-being. We want this building to serve future generations for the next 100 years.

We believe this building is more than an expression of our commitment to sustainability. This building stands as an example of what can be done when you believe yourself to be a steward of the environment. We felt it was up to us to build with conscience so we could guarantee there would be something left for those who come after.

Scope

Before design began the project goals were defined.

- The project must demonstrate the highest level of sustainable design and construction possible. This would be measured through LEED certification.
- The building should demonstrate quality in all aspects.
- Use innovation to solve problems.
- "Walk the talk"—no green washing!
- Assist in changing the local perception of green design through leading by example, outreach, and education.

These goals were added to the desired physical properties of the building and its systems to create the Owner's Project Requirements. As the design progressed, these requirements were translated into the Basis of Design. Each of these documents was then used as a foundation to the commissioning process completed at the end of construction.

Design

The conceptual design called for utilizing the entire site, creating a corporate campus look and feel. The three-story brick building was to be deconstructed, clearing space for a relocated entry to the property and one of two ponds that would serve as

FIGURE 13.1
South-Facing
Sawtooth Addition
Allows for Beneficial
Daylight without
Excessive Solar
Heat Gain

© Debbie Franke Photography, Inc.

retention basins. The manufacturing building would be adaptively reused by using approximately one-third of the existing structure for a parking garage, a portion would be used for a courtyard, and the remaining portion would be used to create two-story office space.

One of the tenants of the Basis of Design was to achieve a minimum of 50 percent energy efficiency in the building. The team chose to use daylight and energy modeling to guide their decisions through design. Early model analysis uncovered a major problem. Five hundred lineal feet of the original structure faced southwest. This orientation created excessive solar heat gain in a proposed design. A "sawtooth" addition to the existing structure was incorporated to align a sun-shaded and heavily glazed south face with a minimally glazed masonry west face. Daylight studies indicated this would allow maximum daylight with minimal heat gain. Mechanical and electrical design-build engineers worked with the project's energy modeler, continuing to guide decisions throughout the design and construction process.

Project

The integrated delivery of this project maximized the synergies between all disciplines, allowing the team to capture the majority of the credit points available within the LEED rating system.

Sustainable Sites

A stormwater management plan was put in place to control 100 percent of the stormwater falling on site, virtually eliminating runoff. This was achieved through a collaborative of design team members and the state's conservation and natural resource departments. The control system starts with a site planted in native prairie grasses combined with micro-detention areas. Runoff from the micro-detention basins are carried by bioswales to forebay structures before delivery to the two retention ponds. The end result of this design allowed for naturally treating all stormwater that does fall on site, eliminating stormwater runoff and site irrigation required by a lawnscape. All site parking was located in the existing structure. The existing roof on that portion of the structure was coated with a soy-based white-colored membrane dramatically reducing the heat island effect caused by roofed and nonroofed surfaces. On-site recycling efforts resulted in 95 percent of the existing brick building being diverted from the landfill.

Architectural and Interior Features

Utilizing the data provided from the energy model, the team incorporated low-E insulated glass with a visual transmittance and shading coefficient that allowed an abundance of natural daylight without the need for window treatments. The insulation within the walls and under the roof was appropriately sized for the energy use targets of the building. An EnergyStar®-rated white roof was installed to reduce heat gain in the summer months. Operable windows were provided for occupants of the building to have control of their thermal comfort and motorized windows were installed in the clerestory to capitalize on natural ventilation during the shoulder months of the year. The thresholds provided in the LEED rating system were used as a minimum starting point when selecting building materials for the project. Materials used in the construction of the building contributed to the team being awarded credit points for recycled content, regionally sourced material, rapidly renewable content, and wood certified by the Forest Stewardship Council. The owner's construction experience provided the opportunity to use salvaged building materials from this and other projects around the area.

Mechanical Systems

In the early design phases of the project the team explored a variety of different systems looking to optimize efficiency while being mindful of the budget. The final solution was innovative use of "state of the shelf" technology. Under-floor air distribution or partial displacement ventilation was used as the platform of the ventilation system. A combination of variable volume air handlers equipped with an energy recovery system, decoupled heating and cooling, demand-based ventilation using carbon dioxide sensors, and natural ventilation capabilities created a system that was energy efficient and provided building occupants control over the thermal conditions at each of their work stations. The raised-access floor system also allowed for integrated power and data distribution, which would reduce "churn" costs after construction was complete.

Electrical Systems

The high-performance glazing systems used to increase the efficiency of the overall building performance was incorporated into the lighting strategy for the building. Reducing the amount of harsh unfiltered natural daylight allowed for a more efficient lighting scheme, resulting in a lighting power density of 0.67 watts per square foot. At the time of construction this was an approximate 50 percent reduction in electrical energy use compared to a normal building. Additional steps were taken to reduce the energy used in the building through daylight-controlled fixtures and occupancy sensors in all multi-use rooms such as bathrooms, copy rooms, conference rooms, and the fitness center. The team also incorporated a 65-kilowatt wind turbine to generate 15 percent of the buildings electric needs through on-site renewable sources.

Plumbing Systems

The combination of low-flow hand lavatories, water-free urinals, and dual-flush water closets were used to reduce the water in the building. A rainwater collection system consisting of a 38,000-gallon underground cistern capturing rainwater from the garage roof provides all water used for sewage conveyance. These efforts resulted in a system that is more than 70 percent more efficient than a conventional building designed to Energy Policy Act of 1992 standards. Solar energy is used to preheat the domestic hot water supply. The system provides 90 percent of the total hot water needs for the building.

Construction Process

During construction the contractor supported the sustainability effort by incorporating the LEED requirements into the new employee orientations. Every person working on the project received an orientation before they were allowed to start work.

The message was reinforced at weekly foreman's meetings and daily toolbox talks. The effort to educate the workers aided in the success of the Construction Waste management and the Indoor Air Quality management programs. Over 90 percent of the total construction and demolition waste was diverted from the landfill. A construction indoor air quality management plan was put in place during the construction process and was also provided for after occupancy took place. This comprehensive plan accounted for low-emitting paints, sealers, caulks, carpet systems, composite wood products, and adhesives.

Lessons Learned

An integrated project delivery is not the easiest delivery method for a project but it can provide outstanding results. In order for this delivery method to be successful, each member of the collective team must understand his or her role as well as all others' roles in the project. In delivering this project we discovered that many people who are familiar with the traditional design/delivery process are uncomfortable when asked to relinquish some of the authority to which they have grown accustomed. We also discovered that many designers are willing to push the limits of design if they are relieved of some of the responsibility. Many of the systems used in this building were smaller than what would be found in a traditional building. The designers were skittish of reducing the equipment size based on past experience and the threat of being held responsible if the owner was not satisfied. The owner of this project was a fully integrated member of the team who knew the importance of pushing the limits and had faith in the team. Once the owner was willing to accept responsibility for the final decision, the designers embraced the challenge and provided a building that was very efficient.

The contractor was also an active partner in the project at the very start. The contractor was asked to be a part of the design team whose input was critically important to the success of the project. During the design phase the contractor provided insight to constructability, cost evaluation of the design, and a source for salvaged materials that could be incorporated into the final design. Contractor support of the process was also witnessed during the construction phase. Including sustainability as a part of the new hire orientations fostered a collaborative atmosphere on the site. Each person working on the site seemed to understand how his or her work could affect the final outcome of the project. It was their support and effort that led to the success of the construction waste management program and the adherence to the indoor air quality protocol put in place. Many of the suggestions brought up during daily toolbox talks were incorporated into the project, which allowed those workers a feeling that they were contributing to the project through something other than the strength of their backs.

The owner learned that a project could be an opportunity to do more than build shade and shelter for employees. The owner used this experience to transform the organization. Many of the things learned while participating in the process were incorporated in day-to-day business after construction was complete. All kitchenettes in the building are equipped with nondisposable plates and cups, as well as dishwashers. Paper and Styrofoam cups are not allowed. A comprehensive office recycling program was created. Housekeeping supplies have been transferred to environmentally friendly alternatives. Print and copy rooms are equipped with printers capable of easy two-sided printing and copying. The grounds are equipped with a half-mile-long fitness trail through the native landscaped grounds.

PROJECT 13

Project type: Institutional/higher education

Project size: 75,000 square feet

Project delivery: Design-bid-build

Project owner: Public

LEED certification: LEED-NCv2.1 Gold

Introduction

In February 2000, a community college contracted a local architect to perform a master plan and design for a new campus for the school system. The citizens of the local community were involved in a series of conversations impacting this master plan study and design of the first building to populate this new campus. The first of the campus buildings serves up to 2,500 students and provide an array of services to the community. The amenities include a multipurpose room for college and community activities, "smart classroom" technologies (Internet access, computer/video/DVD projector, and a document scanner/projector conveniently located at an instructor's work station) in each classroom, recharging stations for electric/hybrid vehicles, and a changing room and shower facility for bike commuters, to name a few. The first building to be constructed on this new campus also provides offices for the college. This area of the county has a long tradition of being environmentally conscious. Thus, the community encouraged and endorsed the vision of the college to develop a sustainable campus. In response to this support, the decision was made to pursue LEED certification. The project emphasized connectivity to the surrounding environment through expansive daylighting and views from classrooms, offices, and the commons.

The team faced several challenges early in the process:

- Schedule: Working through the fall of 2005 into the summer of 2007, the new college was ready for the first day of school on August 20, 2007.
- Definition of the site boundary: While the master plan was developed for the entire campus, the site boundary was limited to the area of construction for the new building. This presented both site design challenges and a unique project boundary. The master plan for the campus calls for as many as seven buildings in total. The funding put in place for this project allowed for the construction of some of the infrastructure needed for the future expansion of the campus. Because the future expansion will take place while this building is in service, the college decided to move forward with the construction of some of the future parking lots in an effort to accommodate material lay-down areas and contractor parking associated with future construction. These lots were not included in the site boundary based on the merit that they were put in place to support future buildings. Furthermore, this strategy allowed for a greater area of the future site to be planted with native vegetation and less site disturbance during the construction of future buildings.
- Proximity of site: The new building had to be built very close to a waterway. While this is not a defined wetland area for LEED purposes, the stream was not to be disturbed during or after construction.
- Weather conditions: Construction for the new building began in the fall of 2005 with completion occurring in May 2007. This forced the construction team to be diligent in the scheduling and delivery of building materials in consideration of the CIAQ program in place during construction.

Scope

The 75,000-square-foot building consists of the following:

- One two-story and one three-story education wing
- A central staircase and student lounge (commons area) that serves as the main entry, gathering place, and dining area for the school—an area designed to welcome students, families, community users, and guests to the school
- Student service center to house the registration/enrollment, counseling, testing/ placement and library functions that support the student community
- A 200-person-capacity multipurpose room

- Art studio, science and computer labs, and an ITV classroom for distance learning
- Administrative and faculty offices

Project

Sustainable Sites

The challenge of working with this site was a tremendous undertaking. However, with every challenge comes opportunity. Because this phase of the campus was to be constructed on a "greenfield" site, the entire infrastructure needed to be put in place. Many of the natural areas were defined through the college's long-term commitment to the community. Included in the design were several strategies to capture credits defined within Sustainable Sites. All areas affected by the construction process were well protected during construction. Bicycle storage racks were placed within 200 yards of an entrance. A locker room and shower facilities were incorporated into the building design as an amenity for all building users. The areas along the north, east, and west site boundaries (20-acres) and the area surrounding a retention pond were restored or preserved, including some old-growth forest, as a commitment to support the efforts to protect open space and limit the development footprint. Extensive stormwater retention focused on one large retention pond along with extensive native vegetation. A specific plant species list was utilized around the retention pond and other restoration areas for filtration of phosphorous and suspended solids. Because of the local climate, the design team incorporated a dual strategy in pursuing the heat island credits. The site photometric study indicates the use of cutoff light fixtures throughout the site to reduce light pollution.

Water Efficiency

Fortunately, the temperate climate and the use of native and adapted plant species allowed the team to eliminate a permanent irrigation system from the site. All grass and plant species are drought-tolerant, which allowed them to survive without permanent irrigation systems. The school decided to use waterfree urinals, low-flow toilets, and low-flow fixtures to achieve a substantial water reduction.

Energy and Atmosphere

The college was keenly interested in reducing its energy bills. This is a climate zone with wide fluctuations from very cold winters to extremely hot and humid summers.

The building was designed with the guidance of extensive energy modeling, with the final design realizing a 30 percent energy cost savings. The lighting power densities were minimized and there are stepped daylighting controls in all classrooms. Motion sensors in the building control both lighting and HVAC operation. The college made a choice to pursue both fundamental and additional building commissioning.

Materials and Resources

The citizens of this area have a strong conservation ethic. The general contractor for the project set out an aggressive program of local sourcing and recycling. This focus has paid off, with over 40 percent of materials being sourced from regional manufacturers and over 95 percent of construction waste diverted from landfills. Care was taken in selecting low-VOC materials such as paints, adhesives, carpets, and composite woods.

Indoor Environmental Quality

The college made a commitment to provide a high standard of indoor air quality and comfort. The design of the HVAC system utilized the ASHRAE Standard 62.1 as the basis of design, and ventilation needs in the building are integrated with CO_2 sensors. No tobacco products are allowed anywhere on the premises, including during the construction phase. A construction indoor air quality management plan was put in place and strictly adhered to during construction. Careful attention was given to protecting HVAC ductwork and other components before and after installation, and building flush-out was completed in June 2007.

Innovation in Design

The goal of becoming the first LEED-NC certified community college building in the state guided the team to a number of innovations on this project. Foremost is the extensive education plan, consisting of a sophisticated informational kiosk and extensive guided tours. Other innovation credits were achieved for the exceptional performance in materials sourcing and construction waste management.

Lessons Learned

As with many public projects, financing for this building was based on fundraising and local community support. The design of this project began many years before the actual construction. At the start of this effort, there was a desire to "go green" but the actual requirements found in the LEED rating system, were not incorporated into the contract documents until the project had been funded. The public nature of the funding for this project also forced a design-bid-build delivery of the project. The competing general contractors were asked to deliver their pricing on bid day. There was a public opening of the bids and the low number was awarded the project. This is not always the best approach for a project seeking LEED certification.

In this situation the successful low bidder sought professional assistance from a sustainability consultant when assembling their estimate. The consultant provided critical information regarding what would be required by the contractor during the procurement and the construction phase of the project. During the review of the bid documents, the consultant identified situations in which the documents did not support the LEED requirements. Prior to finalization of the contract these issues were addressed averting potential problems between what was implied by the documents and what was actually in the documents. The contractor also used this project as an opportunity to learn how to deliver a LEED project. This was the contractor's first LEED project and attention was paid to the processes required for the successful documentation of procurement activities as well as site management of indoor air quality protocols and construction waste management plans.

At the time of award the project was substantially over the original estimate. The contractor was asked to participate in a value engineering exercise in an effort to reduce the overall cost, without diminishing the scope of the project. There were certain "green elements" included in the design that added cost but no other sustainable benefit to the project. The loss of many of these elements was disappointing to the owner. However, this exercise did reduce cost and the team was ultimately awarded a Gold level certification by USGBC.

PROJECT 14

Project type: Industrial/manufacturing
Project size: 1,500,000 square feet
Project delivery: Design-build
Project owner: Private
LEED certification: LEED-NCv2.1 Gold

Introduction

In 2004, this owner made the decision to develop a parcel of existing property located in the northern portion of the Midwest for a new plant location. A design-build team consisting of architect, sustainability consultant, construction manager, and various design-build firms responded to the request for proposal sent out by the owner. In the spring of 2004, the team was awarded a design-build contract for the manufacturing facility. A critical component of the request for proposal was the owner's desire to have this facility designed and constructed as a LEED certified building.

Work on an integrated design began immediately after the official notification to proceed. The team assembled a "design center," which was located in the office space of one of the team members. At the center, owner, architects, engineers, and representatives of the building occupants worked together to develop the final build solution for the project. The expanded team worked together in the design center for eight months, integrating design concepts and sustainable strategies before relocating to the site in the fall of 2004. Some of the major challenges facing the team included:

Definition of the site boundary: Prior to the start of the project, the site supported a functioning facility not associated with this project scope. The construction of the central utility complex and other buildings had begun late in 2003 and was not a part of the team's scope of work. A large percentage of infrastructure was in place prior to the start of the project.

Scope: The scope of work was to design and construct shade and shelter for four distinct building uses: parts assembly, general assembly, administration, and a welcome/arrival center for the complex. A key feature is that this owner divides the responsibility of developing a new facility. There are four basic groups who approach the development from their own respective disciplines. While interrelated, these four groups have their own success criteria and manage their own set of independent contractors.

- o Facilities: Responsible for the creation of the buildings only
- o Process: Responsible for the procurement and start-up of the process equipment and automation used in the manufacturing process
- o Facility Management: Responsible for the manufacturing and operations of the plant
- o Purchasing: Responsible for the purchase of all goods and services at the lowest market price

Additional challenges related to the project's scope were the following:

- o Separation of the teams' scopes of work and unrelated contractors working around the buildings included under this contract
- o Completion of the buildings prior to follow-up contractors who would be responsible for the process equipment housed in the buildings constructed under this contract

Scope

The revised master plan for the complex consists of a parts plant, manufacturing shop (including administration area), central utilities complex, paint shop, central administration building, arrival center, and assembly building. The parts plant was built by a different contractor approximately two years prior to this contract. At the time of award, construction of the central utilities building and paint shop was progressing under the direction of a different contractor. The design-build contractor's scope of work requiring LEED certification consisted of the following:

- Manufacturing shop, including its administration area: This portion of the complex is used to assemble the product prior to painting.
- General assembly shop: This portion of the complex is used for the final assembly of the product.
- Central administration building: This portion of the complex houses the administrative functions that support the entire complex.
- Arrival center: This is to be a flagship complex for the owner. The function of this building is to welcome both employees and guests to the complex. Everyone who visits the complex for any reason will enter through this building.

No process equipment, automation, conveyors, central utilities equipment, or manufacturing process were included in this scope of work. The related scope of the project was submitted to USGBC as a basis of this certification.

Project

The LEED-NC rating system was written for a typical office building; applying it to a manufacturing facility took some innovation and diligence. Another challenge was working on an expansive site with multiple contractors constructing buildings that were not required to be LEED certified. The design-build contractor held responsibility for all site work and required nonexisting infrastructure. For the purposes of the LEED submission, it was imperative to define the scope of this work and that of other general contractors for the requirements of LEED certification.

Sustainable Sites

Because this phase of the complex expansion was to be constructed on a previously developed site, much of the infrastructure existed. Many of the natural areas were defined through the owner's intent and commitment to the community. Bicycle storage racks were placed within 200 feet of the front entrance of the central administration building. A fitness center with locker rooms and showers was incorporated into the building design as an amenity for the employees. Most of the east side of the site was intentionally left undisturbed during construction and contributed to the efforts in the developed footprint credit. The prerequisite of sedimentation and soil erosion control was addressed from the onset of the project. All areas affected by the construction process were well protected during construction and will continue to be protected by the owner during ongoing operations. The owner made a commitment to the local community and this effort plays a major role as part of the wildlife habitat program developed for this location dedicating 34.4 acres of land to be restored in native habitat. An extensive stormwater conveyance system consisting of bioswales, vegetative ditches, and culverts culminating at a constructed "three-gate" sluice gate, which was established during the previous development phase and supported the stormwater control efforts. A specific plant species list was utilized and planted in the ditches and swales for filtration of phosphorous and suspend solids. To reduce the heat island effect attributed to more than 1.5 million square feet of roof surface, a high-albedo roofing material was specified and installed on all buildings.

Water Efficiency

The owner's commitment to use native and adapted plant species allowed the team to eliminate a permanent irrigation system from the site design. All grass and plant species present on site are either native or adapted species and drought-resistant, which allows them to survive without permanent irrigation systems. The team looked for innovation in water reduction to create value for the owner. A rainwater harvesting system based on a cutting-edge roof drain system was utilized in nine out of eleven bathrooms located in the general assembly buildings. The team also used waterless urinals and low-flow fixtures to further their water reduction efforts.

Energy and Atmosphere

This owner believes in extensive commissioning of all building components. The commissioning plan used on this project merged the owner's multipart buyout procedures with the SMACNA's best practices for building systems commissioning. The result of this effort was a thorough inspection and functional test of each piece of equipment installed in this project. The design team started with the requirements of ASHRAE/IESNA Standards to formulate the design. No CFC-based refrigerants were used in the HVAC&R equipment. The ventilation requirements needed in the manufacturing spaces of the buildings challenged the energy optimization of the building systems; nevertheless, strides were made to design in an effort to capture a significant amount of EAc1 points.

Material and Resources

The nature and type of the constructed buildings supported the intent of the Material and Resources section of the rating system. The four buildings are comprised of a steel infrastructure with an insulated metal skin. The thickness of the concrete floors and supporting members all added to both recycled content and the use of local material suppliers. The team sourced a local recycling vendor for all of the construction waste generated throughout the project. Wood, cardboard, metal, and concrete were recycled to the fullest extent. Comingled trash bins were tipped and sorted so any salvageable materials could be diverted from the local landfill.

Indoor Environmental Quality

The owner made a commitment to provide a high standard of workplace health and safety. The design of the HVAC utilized ASHRAE 62.1 as the basis of design. Smoking is not allowed anywhere in the buildings. The manufacturing processes were not included in the scope of the certification. However, the design was required to include the manufacturing load into calculations and documentation. These requirements supported our efforts to achieve ventilation effectiveness, but slightly hindered our energy optimization efforts. The construction indoor air quality program put in place during construction went beyond the suggestions of SMACNA by incorporating a Biological Pollution Prevention Protocol using the best practices guidelines. This extensive CIAQ plan was successfully implemented with the support of all contractors working on site. The efforts made by the team were validated through indoor air quality testing before occupancy. Testing was performed in accordance with the LEED requirements to validate the success of both the CIAQ management and the use of low-VOC materials during construction.

Innovation in Design

The educational process started at the very first partnering session where everyone on the extended design team was introduced to the LEED system. A series of workshops was conducted to further integrate the systems approach to the design of the buildings. Sustainable strategies drove an economic model that funded the rainwater catchment system used in the buildings. The constant attention to specifying and procuring materials allowed us to surpass the intended goals for both recycled content and locally manufactured goods.

Lessons Learned

The contractor working on this project learned a valuable lesson in regard to the use of terms in the Request for Proposal language. The RFP made reference to LEED but was not as specific as the owner had intended. During the discovery stage of the estimating a question was asked as to the level of interest and what should be included in the estimate. A response indicated that the project should be "certifiable." No real definition was provided. After award, the contractor discovered that the owner's intent was to have the project certified. The contractor's estimate did not include all of the effort that would be required to bring the project through the certification process. Fortunately, the contractor was able to negotiate terms with the owner that included the majority, though not all, of the costs associated with the certification effort.

The intent of the owner was to have the project certified. The team was challenged to define what the project was, in order to document the required prerequisites and credits for LEED certification. The contractor used the knowledge of the sustainability consultants to find ways to capitalize on the requirements of the building to find additional credit points that were overlooked early in the conceptual planning phases of the project. This effort enabled the team to deliver a project that was not only certified, but was certified at a Gold level.

Index